Books by André Migot

Thin Edge of the World

THIN EDGE

of the

WORLD

by
André Migot

WITH ILLUSTRATIONS

MAPS BY K. C. JORDAN

LITTLE, BROWN AND COMPANY

BOSTON • TORONTO

Contents

Illustrations appear between pages 150-151.
Maps appear on pages 28, 113, and 131.

Thin Edge of the World

Introduction

I HAVE always loved solitude, and looking back over the years I see that this has been the ruling passion of my life. As a small boy I was forever reading books of travel in the lonely wastes of Central Asia, in polar ice-fields or the silence of a Canadian forest. When I looked out of the window at my schoolmates playing in the dingy narrow streets of one of the old quarters of Paris, I had no wish to join them. I liked to play as much as they did, but I preferred to be on the sands of the Gobi desert or following Scott and Amundsen across the ice. Everyone knows that children love stories of adventure and long to emulate their heroes, but when once they reach the so-called age of reason, they put aside these childish toys and settle down to the serious business of earning a living. Perhaps I have never reached the age of reason. Certainly I have never lost my childish dreams, but have often struggled to realize them. And as to serious things — I must admit I find it hard to take them seriously.

Thin Edge of the World

The first chance I had of making my dreams come true was when I was at the university and a fellow student introduced me to Captain Charcot. This great explorer had already led two expeditions to the antarctic in the *Français* and the *Pourquoi-pas?* and he was one of the gods of my Olympus. He agreed to take me as a doctor and biologist on the new expedition that was then afoot. But the war came to destroy his plans, and Charcot never visited the antarctic again.

It was not until 1952 that I had another chance of going to the antarctic.

My quest for solitude had led me into many strange places in the years between. I had climbed the high Alps. I had spent a year of contemplation in the Cistercian Order, but my spirit did not belong there. I had made two journeys to the Far East and found peace in a Buddhist retreat at Shangu Gompa. And now I had returned to France after seven years in the East, and felt like a foreigner in a strange country.

This interlude between two adventures lasted two months as I visited old friends, interviewed publishers and gathered around me the things which I had brought from China and Tibet. But my little room in Paris was invaded by the din of traffic, thundering buses and the happy shrieks from the school playground next door, which drove out all peace of spirit.

Introduction

Then one afternoon I went to see some old mountaineering friends who keep a shop where one can buy skis and alpenstocks. I found them talking to a tall attractive man who had once been a ski instructor at the Alpine School. His name was Lieutenant Matha. I told him about my journeys, and discovered that he had just spent a year in the Kerguelen Islands. He was preparing to go back there, and he talked for some time about these lonely windswept islands in the far south of the Indian Ocean. This country sounded utterly unlike anything I had ever seen; from what he said of its climate, its landscapes, its birds and its beasts it might have been part of another planet. My interest must have been obvious, for he said:

"The Overseas Ministry is looking for a doctor for the next expedition. Perhaps you might find that an interesting experience. . . ."

I duly applied, and a month later I learned that I was to go. There was a month before I was to leave, but the heavy cargo was to be shipped at once. Besides being the doctor of the expedition I was to be responsible for biological research, so I had to stock up not only with surgical instruments, drugs and dressings — to say nothing of my own personal gear — but also with films and photographic equipment so that I could make a record of the penguins, sea elephants and other interesting fauna. I also had good reason to hope that I should still have enough leisure to work on the mass of Tibetan books, manuscripts and notes which I had brought home from the East but had not begun to edit. I had not even opened the cases. There was only just time to sort out the books and papers that I thought I should want, repack them and get them sent off to Marseilles. There were fifteen packing cases altogether, none of which I could spare if I were not to waste a year's work by going to Kerguelen, but I doubted whether the leader of the expedition would feel they were really necessary to its success. However, he reassured me by insisting that they would hardly be noticed in a cargo of ten thousand tons. All the same I was to suffer a series of headaches when we came to unload them, the first and no doubt the last time that Tibetan manuscripts have ever been landed on Kerguelen.

The Kerguelen Islands form an archipelago in the southern Indian Ocean in what geographers term the subantarctic zone. This is the band encircling the Southern Hemisphere between 40° and 50° south; its special features are the temperature of the water on the surface of the ocean and the prevalent westerly winds. Together they create a peculiar and vile climate.

As the antarctic explorer journeys south he crosses

Introduction

two lines known as the lines of convergence, which are
recognized by a sudden drop in the temperature of the
surface water. On the first of these boundaries the cooler
and therefore denser water of the subantarctic zone (50°
F. in summer) sinks below the warm (60° to 70° F.)
subtropical water. This sharp change marks the traveler's
entry into the subantarctic zone. When at last he reaches
the antarctic proper, there is a second convergence, and
the cold antarctic waters (38° F. in summer and 30.5°
F. in winter) sink below the less frigid subantarctic
waters. And in this subantarctic zone, known to the old
sailors as the "roaring forties," the westerly gales howl
almost incessantly, raising waves from thirty to fifty feet
high.

The two islands upon which our mission was based are
at opposite ends of this zone, New Amsterdam (37° 52′
south) being at the extreme north and even a little outside the convergence, while the Kerguelen Islands extend
from 48° 27′ to 50° south, right on the antarctic convergence. As a result the two islands suffer very different
climates. And Heard Island, the nearest Australian base,
is well inside the antarctic zone.

All these islands are very far apart, small points hardly
visible in the vast expanse of the Indian Ocean. They
are a long way from any shipping routes. Aircraft cannot land on them because of the unceasing and violent

gales. They are 1900 miles from Madagascar, the nearest inhabited country, 2300 from Australia and 2600 from South Africa. But the antarctic continent is only 1200 miles away. They are without doubt the loneliest and most isolated islands in the world.

In order to explain the function of our mission I must say something of the history of the Kerguelen Islands. The exploration of the southern seas was dominated for three centuries by the myth of the *terra australis incognita*, a fabulous land which the ancient Greeks assumed must exist to counterbalance the regions of the Northern Hemisphere that were gradually emerging from the unknown. The few islands that were discovered were thought to be the outposts of this continent. Geographers compared them to the Garden of Eden, and in 1505 the Sieur de Gonneville wrote a detailed account of his sojourn of six months "in the Third World otherwise called the Austral, Meridional, Antarctic and Unknown Land," a rich and populous region of which he had taken possession. This land was in fact Brazil, but Louis XV overlooked this detail when he ordered the Chevalier Yves de Kerguelen-Trémarec, a Breton captain, to visit the southern continent and ascertain what advantage could be derived from it.

And so, on February 12, 1772, two vessels of the Royal

Introduction

French Fleet, the *Fortune* and the *Gros-Ventre*, commanded by Captain de Kerguelen, sighted an unknown island. They had put out from the Île de France (now known as Mauritius) on January 16, heading for the south. After crossing latitude 40° south and sailing for several days through thick sea mists and storms of snow and sleet, they anchored before this unknown coast. The next morning the fog had lifted and they were astonished to find a great expanse of land before their eyes. But Kerguelen was prevented by bad weather from completing his task. On February 18 he lost sight of land and also of his other ship, the *Gros-Ventre*, but he knew that she was well provisioned, so he turned the *Fortune* round and sailed her back to the Île de France to repair some damage she had suffered. Meanwhile the *Gros-Ventre* managed to lower a boat, and her captain, de Boiguehenneuc, succeeded in landing in an inlet, which he named Sea Lion Cove. It is still inhabited by sea elephants, but is today called Gros-Ventre Cove. After annexing the territory in the name of the King, he departed and returned to France.

Kerguelen was graciously received by His Majesty, to whom he gave the following account:

The lands which I have had the good fortune to discover seem to constitute the central mass of the continent — the fifth continent of the world — and the region which I have

named South France is situated in such a manner as to domi-
nate India, the Moluccas, China and the South Seas. It ex-
tends ENE and offers varying temperatures and climates
for settlement by our compatriots. . . . South France will
henceforth give a new existence to the Île de France and
Bourbon. It will increase their commerce and wealth three-
fold and provide the settlers in those tropical islands with
the provisions and products to which they were accustomed
in their native climate and which they cannot do without.
There is no doubt that we shall find in the new continent
timber, mines, diamonds, rubies, semiprecious stones, marble.
. . . An isolated continent which has never been in commu-
nication with the rest of the world should be able to throw a
wonderful light on the process of evolution on our globe.
Even if we do not find there men of a different species to our
own, we shall at least find natural human beings, living in a
primitive state, free from defiance and remorse and ignorant
of the artifices of civilized man. In fact South France will
furnish a wonderful exhibition of moral and physical speci-
mens.

This owes more to a power of imagination unusual in
a Breton, and to Rousseau's doctrine of the Noble Savage, than to exact observation; for in fact he had only
had a passing and distant glimpse of the land in misty
weather. King Louis XV could hardly remain unmoved
by the prospect of such a profitable colony, and he decided to send a new expedition to these Fortunate Isles.
On October 29 of the same year Kerguelen again set

out from the Island of Bourbon with a flotilla of three ships, the *Roland*, *L'Oiseau* and *La Dauphine*. On December 14 they sighted the islands, and spent the rest of the month exploring the northwest coast. Kerguelen in the *Roland* was unable to land because of storm and fog, but on January 6 de Rochegude, one of the officers of *L'Oiseau*, managed to get ashore and claim Kerguelen as French territory.

Two days later Captain de Kerguelen was obliged to put about and return to France because his men were so ravaged with scurvy. It was an inglorious homecoming; he had lost all his illusions.

I have surveyed some twenty leagues of these coasts and have reason to believe that the whole circumference of the islands measures two hundred leagues. It seems quite clear that this region is as barren as Iceland and even more uninhabitable and uninhabited.

The reality indeed fell short of the dream and, naturally, Kerguelen was as much blamed for the reality as he had been praised for the dream. Ugly rumors went about. He should never have abandoned the *Gros-Ventre* during his first voyage. What was he doing with the Governor of Bourbon's wife and daughter on board the *Roland?* And his officers were jealous because of poor Louison, a pretty girl he had smuggled on board at Brest for his own pleasure. He was condemned to prison — not the somber Bastille but a pleasant little château near Saumur. He was still there when the revolution broke out, and since he was plainly one of the King's victims he was set at liberty, advanced in rank and appointed manager of the port at Brest, where he remained until his death in 1797.

He had done little more than to discover the islands. La Paute, a member of the Academy who sailed in *L'Oiseau*, took a few meteorological observations and drew a map on which one can recognize a few of the places, some of which preserve their original names today.

Two years later Captain James Cook called at Kerguelen during his third journey round the world. On Christmas Day 1776 his two vessels, *Resolution* and *Discovery*, entered Oiseau Bay, and he christened his anchorage Christmas Harbor. He remarked in his log, "I could have very properly called the island Desolation Island to signalize its sterility but in order not to deprive M. de Kerguelen of the glory of having discovered it, I called it Kerguelen Land." Cook and his companions have left a description of some twenty plants peculiar to the island, most of the birds and some of the more conspicuous headlands. His map, moreover, is more exact and more detailed than Kerguelen's.

Introduction

The islands were further explored by James Clark Ross with the *Erebus* and *Terror* in 1840, and by no less than five scientific expeditions in 1874. Two of these expeditions were British, two German and one American; three of them had come to observe the transit of Venus, which had also been one of Cook's objects in the Southern Hemisphere.

In 1893 the French Government sent the dispatch boat *Eure* to hoist the tricolor and reaffirm French sovereignty. Scientific expeditions continued to visit the islands, but no Frenchman took any great interest in them until the brothers Rallier du Baty charted the coast in 1908 – 1909 and 1913 – 1914. Many other explorers made studies of Kerguelen, M. Aubert de la Rüe's work being perhaps the most important.

Meanwhile whalers and sealers had exploited the islands since the beginning of the nineteenth century. The sea elephants proved to be an easier prey than whales or seals. The sealers landed their flat-bottomed boats in the smallest inlets, and proceeded to massacre every sea elephant they could lay their hands on, not even sparing the pregnant females. Then the oil was boiled out of their dismembered carcasses in huge caldrons. Even the penguins were put to practical use. Their bodies were crushed in a press to extract the oil, and the remaining mass of shattered bones and feathers was used to feed the fire below the boiling caldrons. One still finds traces of this ghastly trade on the islands: ruined huts, mallets for clubbing defenseless sea elephants, presses and caldrons, and sometimes a tombstone with the name almost worn away.

This free-for-all was brought under some sort of control at the end of the nineteenth century, when the Boissière brothers formed the Compagnie Générale des Îles Kerguelen. The slaughter of sea elephants was finally ended in 1931 by a fall in the price of oil. Meanwhile the Boissières had prospected for minerals and tried to raise sheep, but after a promising start the beasts sickened and died, while the colonists quarreled until one of them came to a violent end. In spite of these failures, France continued to take an interest in the islands until 1940, and during the war several German raiders were based on Kerguelen.

After the war France was obliged to occupy the islands in order to retain her sovereignty over them. According to modern international law, it is not enough merely to discover virgin territory and plant a flag on it; the land must be occupied and administered. Moreover, there was not a single meteorological station in the southern Indian Ocean; the International Organization of Civil Aviation called upon France to install such stations, and it was agreed to do so. Eventually, at the end of 1949, a mission was sent out to Kerguelen to reaffirm French sover-

Introduction

eignty, to establish a permanent base and meteorological
station, to see whether it was practicable to build an air
base, to investigate the possibility of re-establishing the
sealing trade and to carry out biological and geological
research. It was to this mission that I was now going.

CHAPTER ONE

From Paris
to the Kerguelen Islands

DECEMBER 7, 1952. At last the great day came. At
five o'clock in the morning (all the long-distance
airplanes start at an unearthly hour) a taxi carried me
through the blackness of the night to the air terminal,
where I found a group of other "Southerners." I knew
most of them already, but there were a few strange faces,
for instance that of Père Menu, a young Dominican
father who was the chaplain to the mission as well as
being the hospital attendant. In the latter capacity he
would come under my supervision, and I had insisted
that he should be told to take a practical course in a hospital if he was to justify his appointment, but he told me
quite calmly that he had not had time to do so. I was
too busy registering my somewhat bulky baggage to
worry much over this first disappointment. Soon we

were in the coach driving to Orly, where we went through the last formalities, showing our vaccination certificates, interviewing officials and posing for flash-light photos. Next day our group would appear in the papers under the heading OFF TO THE ENDS OF THE EARTH — more grist for the journalists.

At ten o'clock the mist lifted as we were flying over the range dominated by Mont Blanc. I crammed my face to the window to gaze at the most glorious landscape we should see on our whole voyage. The aircraft was not very high above the great mass of mountains, and the summits seemed almost level with us. I knew the region so well that I recognized all the details of the scene. We followed fairly closely along the Argentière glacier, skirting the wonderful rock wall with its peaks Les Drus, La Verte, Les Droites and Les Courtes. Further to the right we saw the long spine of the ridge leading by the Little and the Great Jorasses to Mont Blanc. We were so near that I was able to make out every landmark along the routes which I had often climbed slowly and pain-fully. My heart was full of wonderful memories. That morning we flew over the mountain even more easily than the eagles I had so often envied when I trudged on foot. The sky was marvelously clear, with a few lovely white clouds floating round the crest of Mont Blanc, which seemed to have been placed there just to please the eye of the beholder. But the glorious vision lasted only a few minutes, and it soon was lost behind the mists that arose from the Paduan plains.

I was disappointed to find the airports so utterly dull. I had hoped that the Athens airfield, which we reached late in the day, would offer me a splendid view of the Acropolis glowing in the fires of the setting sun, but it is very far from the city, and there was nothing to see but a depressingly ordinary bunch of huts. Soon it was night, and all the way to Cairo there was nothing to catch the eye but the curious sight of a cluster of little lights on the Egyptian coast. After a dull dinner in the stifling restaurant at Almaza, we flew nonstop to Djibouti, where we arrived in the middle of the night, jaded and sleepy. No one can pass through Djibouti without stocking up with American cigarettes, cigars, ball-point pens and a hundred others things which they seem to be able to sell at lower prices than anywhere else in the world. We succumbed to these temptations and drank lemonade and lukewarm Coca-Cola until we transferred to the stuffy cabin of another airplane, graced by a new air hostess no less charming than the last.

Dawn rose on a landscape that looked as if the last day had come — a yellow desert, burned up, desiccated, crinkled, crevassed and full of craters like the surface of the moon, without a stream, a lake or a tree. Not a village, not a man, not a camel was visible, nothing but tracks climbing the tawny mountainsides and dropping down into tawny ravines. They came from nowhere and went nowhere. This was Somaliland, but whether Italian, French or British I couldn't tell. It didn't seem to matter to whom such ghastly desolation belonged. Soon we were over the sea, and it was a relief to have left the wilderness behind us.

We were now about to cross the equator, and those of us who had not crossed it before — that is to say, most of the party — prepared to be officially baptized. The ceremony was more modest than those rites on board ship, when Neptune appears in his crown of silver paper, with his courtiers and trumpeters, clad in tinseled robes and wearing beards of tow. We had to forego the ritual bath and the customary horseplay. In the little cabin of our aircraft the ceremony had quite a different character. It was discreet, summary and refined. The blond air hostess was mistress of ceremonies, much preferable to the usual tarry Neptune with his smelly beard. We knelt in turn before this attractive goddess, who sprinkled us discreetly with Évian water and then offered us a glass of champagne. Some of us were even favored with a kiss on the forehead. Our young chaplain was one of the lucky ones. He did not seem particularly put out, and we were all delighted. At the end of the show we each received a certificate to prove that we had entered the Southern Hemisphere.

With all these distractions we crossed the wide expanse of the Indian Ocean to Madagascar without being bored. At last we began to lose height over the hills of red earth and the dark forests of the high Antananarivo plateau, which reminded me of the Dalat region, over which I had often flown in Indochina. We lunched at the airdrome at Arivoniman, and then drove by coach to Antananarivo, where rooms had been reserved.

I was agreeably surprised by the climate in this large town. It was already the middle of summer and the days were often stormy, but up on this high plateau (five thousand feet) the air was fresh and pleasant. We were staying only a few days there, and I determined to make the most of them. I was lucky enough to find a friend from Indochina, who took me on some interesting trips into the country. We spent the last two days at Tamatave, which has a beautiful beach; but I did not like the place, which was much hotter than Antananarivo, and our quarters were uncomfortable. We were glad to leave it on December 16, when our ship, the *Vercors*, sailed for the south. The port faded into the distance under a low leaden sky through which heavy storm clouds rolled.

On the eighteenth we called at Port Louis in the island of Mauritius. The town was a great change from Tamatave. With its little Chinese and Indian shops, it is much more like a Far Eastern port than an African town. I spent the day on shore, and in the evening took some of my companions to a Chinese restaurant, where I was glad to find, though much watered down, the tang of the Far East which has got into my blood. I felt as if I had left it only yesterday, and my interlude of several months in France seemed distant and unreal. We were back on board by ten o'clock, and soon afterwards the *Vercors* got under way and headed south. We had left our last port.

Four days later we had already crossed the latitude of Durban. The sea was fairly high, and we were rolling comfortably. The weather was freshening, and the thermometer had fallen to 40° F. Everyone on board had packed away his summer clothes and put on the thick woolen suits with which we were well provided. We seemed to have left the heavy tropic clouds behind. The sky was clear, the sea a deep blue, and the sun made its first appearance since Madagascar, shining with a pure brilliance. That night, in a clear starry sky, the Southern Cross showed itself for the first time, guiding us on our way and luring us towards the icebound regions of the distant southern continent.

By this time life on board had been thoroughly organized, but when sixty passengers have to be crammed into a cargo boat which normally carries twenty, she has to be made into a sort of barracks, which was very distasteful to some of us. It meant that the mission's various social elements were separated from one another, the administrative, military, radio-meteorological and technical branches of our party being sealed into almost watertight compartments. These compartments were fortunately not kept hermetically sealed for the whole of the journey, and a door might sometimes be opened to admit sympathetic individuals from other pens, but generally they were kept closed until we reached Port-aux-Français. All this caused a lot of trivial difficulties and misunderstandings and encouraged friction and personal antipathies.

In order to find room for all the passengers, extra cabins had been built on deck before the ship left Marseilles, each with room for six passengers. These were reserved for those members of the mission known as the senior staff, a term which I greatly disliked. They included the heads of the different services, the officers, the chaplain, the doctors, the scientists and so on. The administrators were given normal cabins. As for the rest of the team — the technicians, soldiers, skilled workmen and Madagascans — they had to put up with the crew's quarters and a dormitory set up in the 'tween-decks. No doubt everyone got what he deserved and had no real reason to complain of his lot, but all the same there were great differences in the comfort and the kind of service different ranks received and in the kind of life they led. This naturally emphasized the distinction between the classes, and strengthened the internal solidarity of each group to the detriment of the community. There were several distinct team spirits where there should have been only one.

The ship did not only have to accommodate human passengers. The *Vercors* was a curious place — half barracks and half farmyard, a sort of modern Noah's Ark. The deck was cluttered up with pens for sheep, pigs and a few cows destined for the little farm at Port-aux-Français. There were also a henhouse and some coops for geese and ducks. Every morning we were awakened by cocks crowing and sheep bleating, which began long before the soldiers' reveille. During the day the fowls and ducks were let out on deck and played happily round in a great heap of hay that had been provided for them. They were joined by some enchanting little black curly lambs that had been born during the voyage and knew no pasture but the deck of the ship. The shepherd walked round among his peaceful little charges doling out food and water, helped in his work by a few passengers who were glad to enjoy these country pleasures in the middle of the ocean.

Thin Edge of the World

We had a very bad time on Christmas Eve. It came on to blow hard, and soon we were in the middle of a full-sized gale, our first since we had left Madagascar. The speed of the wind was not less than ninety miles an hour, and the sea was very high, with waves fifty feet from trough to crest. The ship rolled from side to side, and those bolder spirits who continued to frequent the ward-room found that meals had become exercises in juggling and acrobatics as they tried to catch the glasses, bottles, plates and dishes which skated merrily from one end of the table to the other. There was now no doubt that we were in the Southern Ocean, the home of the "brave winds," and we were beginning to realize how hard they could blow.

Towards evening the weather improved, and our chaplain was able to celebrate midnight Mass in less savage weather. The 'tween-decks had been carefully arranged and decorated and the bunks had been tucked out of the way, but the ceremony seemed very incongruous against this barracklike background in the midst of a heavy swell. The supper which followed the Mass was even less conventional, and our songs and choruses tended to be ribald rather than liturgical. Father Menu took part in the festivity without flinching, although he must have been disconcerted to find that a celibate Christmas could be so unmonastic. I could not help feeling that a year

among these soldiers would complete his religious educa-
tion in a way that he did not expect.

On Christmas Day we crossed the line of the subtropical convergence and sailed into the subantarctic zone.
The temperature of the surface water, which on the
previous night had been 62° F., had fallen in a few hours
to 46° F. and would soon be down to 39° F., the average
sea temperature in summer round the coast of Kerguelen.
The air temperature likewise dropped, and the gusty
wind was unpleasantly cold. We were glad to keep to
our cabins and write our letters home so that they could
go back to Madagascar when the ship returned.

The life in these communal cabins is not easy to describe. My own was calm, for my two cabinmates, Dr.
Pruche, the doctor attached to the New Amsterdam mission, and Captain Peretti, were peaceful companions, but
other cabins were less serene. It so happened that Father
Menu had to share a cabin with Chastain the botanist, a
charming and fastidious man, but spiritually the very reverse of our chaplain; Baltenberger the geophysicist, a
silent and apparently peaceful Alsatian; and Savin d'Orfond, the administration officer, cultivated, ironical and
full of good stories. Chastain and Baltenberger had been
inoculated against typhoid and were thoroughly under
the weather. This seemed to exaggerate their normal
characters. Baltenberger became even more taciturn, and

Chastain more witty and sarcastic; he squatted on his bed
with the sheets wound round him so that he looked like
Gandhi, and railed at everything and everybody. Poor
Savin was laid up in bed with a painful attack of lumbago, while Father Menu set out his chasubles with
Olympian calm. To complete this bizarre picture I was
giving Savin d'Orfond a course of acupuncture, and the
cabin looked like a scene from Grand Guignol as it
heaved with the swell, and was crammed with books,
liturgical ornaments and miscellaneous gear, in the middle of which lay a naked man with a forest of Chinese
needles in his back.

I awoke on the twenty-sixth to find that we had run
into fog. The sea had gone down and the wind was less
cold. At about eight o'clock we began to make out the
low-lying coast of the Courbet Peninsula, and soon afterwards the *Vercors* sailed through the Passe Royale into
Morbihan Bay. The entrance to this huge bay, in which
a whole fleet could lie at anchor, is strikingly beautiful,
and the scenery is very wild. The fog began to lift and
the coastline could be clearly seen, indented like a piece
of jigsaw puzzle, and then the fjords, countless islands
and mountains of the archipelago. There stood Pouce,
Wyville Thomson and the Château range, still showing
white patches of snow. In the far distance, thirty-seven
miles away, rose Mount Ross, the highest peak in the

island, which, although it is only 6450 feet high, looks just like one of the higher Alps, with its great glaciers and lofty ice-glazed cliffs.

Soon our base came into view. We blew three blasts on the siren as a salute, and the garrison on land replied with a salvo from their mortars. At half-past eleven the *Vercors* anchored off Port-aux-Français a mile and a half from the shore, for the water is too shallow for a ship to come nearer. The motor launch *Gros-Ventre*, named after Kerguelen's ship, came out to meet us with a motor landing craft which had originally been called the *Galli-portain*, but usually went by a coarser name on account of her noisy exhaust. Mouzon, the chief of the mission, with several other members of the 1952 team, was on board. From the ship the base did not look very cheerful, with its long gray hutments merging into the ground on which they were built, but it was larger than I had expected.

I was one of the first landing party, and as soon as lunch was over we embarked on the *Gallipetant*, which carried us to the shore, deafening us with the sound that came from her stern. I was very moved to set foot for the first time on this island where I was to stay for a whole year. My first gloomy impression of the base was not improved by the reception we got when we landed. For there was nobody to receive us. The station seemed to be deserted.

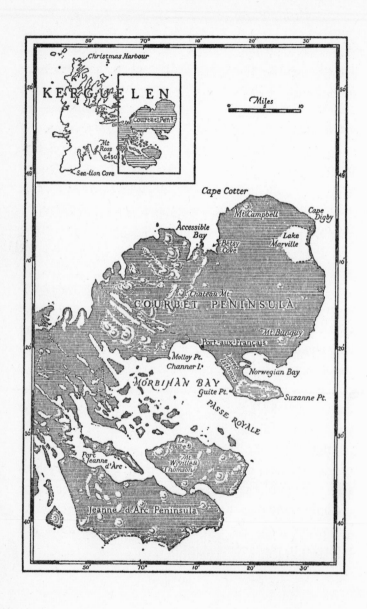

Christmas Harbour

KERGUELEN

Miles

0	5	10

Courbet Pen?

Mt
Ross
6450

Sea-lion Cove

Cape Cotter

Mt Campbell

Cape
Digby

*Accessible
Bay*

Lake
Marville

*Betsy
Cove*

Chateau Mt

C O U R B E T   P E N I N S U L A

Mt Bunguy

Port-aux-Français

Molloy Pt.
Channer I.

Norwegian Bay

M O R B I H A N   B A Y
Guite Pt.

Suzanne Pt.

P A S S E   R O Y A L E

Le
Pouce
Mt.
Wyville
Thomson

Port
Jeanne
d'Arc

Jeanne d'Arc Peninsula

From Paris to the Kerguelen Islands

There was no one waiting for us on the dock, and I walked alone, and rather sadly, across the three hundred yards of sloping acaena grass between the shore and the buildings. No one greeted me except the sea elephants, which sprawled in the grass like young calves and grunted hoarsely as I passed. I saw a few people around the large cookhouse, but they looked very busy and paid no attention to me. At last, after wandering for a while around the camp, I came upon the hospital and found my predecessor, Dr. Baixe, medical officer to the 1952 mission, sitting in an armchair in his room.

He received me very kindly and showed me the hospital and the room which I was to occupy. We soon began to talk familiarly, as two doctors usually will, but before long the conversation came around to the subject which was closest to his heart, that is to say, the petty scandals of the mission and his personal squabbles with the officials. Naturally I did not understand much of what he said because I did not yet know any of the people he was talking about, but during the next few days I had plenty of opportunities of hearing in all their details every possible version of the fantastic stories which seemed to be the only thing that these poor fellows were interested in. I hastened to escape from this flood of grievances and returned to the landing stage.

The place had suddenly come to life. Unloading had already started, and a bustling crowd of men and vehicles flooded the docks. Jeeps, trucks, tractors and weasels were coming and going between the shore and the station, driving at top speed through a cloud of dust. In the midst of this bustle and orgy of internal-combustion engines, the camp with its rut-scored roads, its wooden shanties and its floodlights seemed more like a little American town in the West than the peaceful base which I had pictured.

Unloading the ship is a most unpleasant time for everyone. Calm days are rare, and then the men toil feverishly, before the weather breaks again and makes work impossible. They are up at four in the morning and do not knock off till ten at night, taking time off for their meals in rotation. Often they go on far into the night under the great floodlights. They are strained and anxious, and then small accidents are apt to happen, as I saw from the sick list.

At first we were favored with really splendid weather, and it looked as if the unloading would be finished in record time, if only the wind held off. After all the days spent in the air and on the sea I felt immensely happy to be in beautiful mountain scenery again, and to walk upon grass, go where I liked, and breathe the fresh and invigorating air, which was such a pleasant change from the sultry, stormy heat of Tonkin, where I had spent the summer.

I realized how easy it would be for me to retire from the suffocating promiscuity of camp life and be alone in this new landscape, which I was already beginning to love and understand. A quarter of an hour's walk took me out of sight of the hollow where the camp lay, with its huts like a concentration camp and clouds of yellow dust rising from its roads, and out of earshot of the hum of the electric station and the roar of trucks and bulldozers. Once across the line of low hills which surrounded the station, one seemed far from the world of men, in a new universe, among friendly and peaceful animals, in a land-scape of rugged beauty, with much to feast the mind, the eye and the spirit in spite of its apparent monotony.

I lost no time in making the acquaintance of Aubert de la Rüe and his wife. They gave me a very friendly reception in their primitive dwelling. It was all they had been able to obtain, but Madame Aubert had managed to make their poor little shanty as comfortable as possible. They lived in a remote corner of the station, where they were at any rate alone and quiet, and could work undisturbed. They showed me their splendid collection of photographs, and while we were having tea they told me a great deal about this island where they had lived for two years. They knew it intimately, having walked hundreds of miles exploring it in every direction. Although they were obviously embittered, and with some justification, by the unsympathetic way they had been treated by some of the high officials, I saw through their natural reserve that they had a deep love for this austere and thankless land, where they had suffered much but also found great happiness. Aubert de la Rüe took me for several walks in the country around the camp, showing me round his estate, as it were, and introducing me to the animals and plants of Kerguelen, which he has some right to claim as his own.

I soon found that Desolation Island, as Cook had called it, was true to its reputation. The first two days of sun and calm ended with the sort of bang one might expect from this country of contrasts. The men had been hard at work unloading since the crack of dawn when suddenly at ten o'clock the wind burst upon us. In a few minutes it was blowing at ninety miles an hour. An inflated rubber raft, towed by a motorboat which had just left the jetty, was swept onto the rocks in the little bay of Port-aux-Français and was very nearly lost.

A few moments later the storm caused another accident which very nearly had tragic results. A rubber raft full of packing cases and manned by a couple of men was lying alongside the *Vercors*. They had almost finished loading up when a sudden violent squall broke the moorings and swept the raft out to sea at top speed. Before anyone could do anything to help, it was swept out towards the Passe Royale, and soon disappeared in the thick curtain of spindrift blown into the air from the tops of the waves. If in its mad career the raft had got through the channel, even the *Vercors* would have had small chance of picking it up in such bad visibility. It would soon have been smashed to pieces by the waves, and the men's fate would have been a foregone conclusion. All this happened in a few minutes, but luckily the accident had been seen from the shore, and the *Gros-Ventre* at once put out to chase the fleeing raft. Dr. Pruche, of the New Amsterdam mission, was at the tiller. The doctor's practice at home is in Ushant and he is almost more of a sailor than a medical man. We watched him disappear behind the high waves and were much relieved when he returned, drenched but happy, with the two men, whom he had just managed to overtake and rescue. He could not save the raft, which had vanished in the storm, but it was found a few days later cast up on the beach near Guite Point, having run into a mass of seaweed which prevented it from being carried out to sea.

While we were all alarmed by these accidents, I had some more trivial worries of my own. As the cargo was being precariously ferried ashore I kept thinking of my

fifteen boxes full of notes, books and Tibetan manuscripts. My companions, who knew what store I set by
these precious boxes, used to take a malicious pleasure in
telling me that they had fallen into the sea. There were
few amusements at Kerguelen and to tease me occasionally was not a crime. Though I knew they were probably pulling my leg, I could not help being a little worried every time they told me the bad news, because such
things did happen and the accident to the raft was hardly
reassuring. But the Tibetan gods took good care of my
treasures, which eventually arrived safe and sound.

The bad weather, which held up unloading, had one
advantage. It gave the overworked men time to rest and
the members of the two missions were able to get to
know one another, for hitherto we had all been far too
busy to do so. The period when the ship is unloading is
the busiest and most lively time in the whole year; it is
also the time when the camp is most crowded, for it has
to find room for twice the usual number of people.
There were beds in every hut, and our little hospital,
which had been turned into a guest house, was full of
unaccustomed activity. We also had the rare pleasure of
entertaining a lady. This was because M. Fiasson, a veter-
inary surgeon, had temporarily joined the mission at
Madagascar. He had come on a round trip in the *Vercors*
in order to study an epidemic of cattle disease which had

broken out in New Amsterdam. He was accompanied by his wife, a dynamic young woman, adventurous and very attractive, who had already taken part in interesting expeditions up the Amazon and who was taking advantage of her journey in the *Vercors* and her visits to Kerguelen and New Amsterdam to make a documentary film.

The relations between the two missions were full of surprises. We who had just arrived from France found the attitude and reactions of the team we had come to relieve very puzzling, and also alarming in their implications about our own future. It was clear that a year of isolation at Kerguelen, where fifty men were shut up in a sort of multiple solitary confinement, must have a strong effect on the character and behavior of the most normal people, but it did seem to us that the members of the outgoing mission had let their eccentricity get the better of them and were on even worse terms with one another than most human beings in closed groups.

This eccentricity appeared in the shape of odd motley garments with patches of different colors, ragged socks, flowing beards and leonine manes falling onto the shoulders in Pre-Raphaelite curls or in great tangled mops. This made some of our predecessors look strange or even alarming. Fortunately they could be restored to normal by a few snips of the barber's scissors. It was not so easy to dispose of the web of cock-and-bull stories we had heard since we came. I was the new medical officer, and so every evening I had to endure a spate of gossip about my predecessor, Dr. Baixe, from his cronies or his enemies, all trying to rope me into their feud. It was all the same to me, for I was quite ignorant of the facts, but I could not help sympathizing strongly with the doctor's cause when his faction regaled me with a certain old *marc* from the back of the bin, which the good Dr. Baixe had received from home, and with other small delicacies which had come over in the *Vercors*.

These men, who had certainly been on the best of terms when they set out from France, had reached the point where they hated one another with all their hearts and were divided into factions that were more rigid and bitterly opposed than any savage tribes in Central Africa. Many of them were no longer on speaking terms, and among this group of fifty men living together in the same camp there were some who would communicate with one another only by registered letter. Our ears were stuffed with improbable stories about documents stolen and then discovered in suspicious circumstances, people being searched and summoned, official reports and so on, the drift of these contradictory tales naturally depending on which clique

was telling the story. All this seemed incredibly childish to us, and no doubt the people who were then so
bitter would think so, too, today, but after a whole
year spent in the concentration-camp atmosphere of the
base they really believed their own stories and some of
them had reached the verge of persecution mania. If I
dwell on these feuds it is not because of the facts they
were based on, which were quite trivial, but because
they show how people's minds work when they are isolated in small groups, and because there was a lesson to
be drawn by those in charge of missions such as ours.

There was another lesson to be learned — which we
unfortunately learned much too late — namely, that all
confined groups of people behave in this way, and that
it was by no means peculiar to the outgoing mission.
One need only read any account of an expedition to distant lands. When we arrived at Kerguelen our hearts
were innocent and we were blithely ignorant of the
kind of life we should have to lead. Thus we were in-
clined to judge our predecessors' behavior too severely.
We thought, quite wrongly, that we were different; our
mission seemed to be a model of its kind and its members proof against the errors into which the others had
fallen. Certain petty incidents during our voyage, certain incompatibilities of character and temperament
which were already clear enough, should have made us

more prudent and less cocksure that we should remain a happy Utopian mission. It took us a year to discover our mistake and the folly of our illusions.

During all this time the unloading of the ship continued according to the whims of the calm and stormy weather. On the whole we had more good days than bad. On January 5 at noon it was completely finished, and every man had worked to the limit of his powers. The two teams met for the last time for a celebration dinner, where there was a lavish supply of good wine, songs and gay conversation. The last letters were posted, the inventories of each service were completed, typed, initialled and registered — a formidable task which the chiefs of every service dreaded. The outgoing team's luggage was carried on board. At five o'clock the team embarked on the landing craft which took them to the ship, and at half past six the *Vercors* weighed anchor, sailed round Chaner Island as tradition prescribes, and then headed for the Passe Royale. We were alone, left to ourselves for a whole year.

CHAPTER TWO

Fifty Men on a Desert Island

I MUST now describe the base at Port-aux-Français, where we were to spend a year, and explain how we lived and what we did.

The base is built at the head of a narrow sheltered inlet. The chief accommodation for the mission consists of two large buildings made of specially fireproofed wood, about one hundred and fifty feet long and twenty-five feet wide, which run parallel to the shore some three hundred yards from the sea. They stand slightly above sea level, with a sloping sward of acaena grass lying below them. Building A is the base's heart, or rather its stomach, for it contains the cookhouse, full of modern equipment, the bakery and a large dining hall, which serves also as a games room and a library for books and phonograph records. The rest of the building is divided into twenty private rooms, comfortably furnished, with central heating and hot and cold water. There are also a large washroom fitted with showers, and a darkroom.

Building B contains a large meeting hall and the administrative offices. Instead of single rooms there are a number of small apartments, called "family flats," though up to now they have been inhabited only by single men. Each of these consists of a bedroom, an office, a kitchen and a bathroom. The rest of the building is occupied by the hospital. It is very well equipped, with a consulting room, a modern operating theater with rooms for sterilization and radiography, a biological laboratory, ultraviolet-ray lamps, a well-stocked dispensary, private rooms for the medical officer and the chaplain, three wards for patients, and a bathroom. There is central heating everywhere, with electric radiators and a hot-water system.

Besides these two large buildings there are several annexes, so that altogether the camp forms a little village more comfortable and up to date than most hamlets in France. In the center stands a large building for the radio and meteorological station. It is the only building of more than one story and has large bay windows so that it can be used as a sort of watchtower to make observations of the weather. The radio station on the ground floor is very busy, since it is also a post office, where we can send messages to our families. The ration is twenty-five words a week.

There are also prefabricated Fillod huts used for soldiers' billets, workshops, garages and stores. Lastly there is a powerful central electric generating station, working day and night. Great care is taken to maintain the fire posts, for those in charge of the base are constantly anxious about the danger of fire. With so many wooden buildings jammed so close together and a wind which never stops blowing in Kerguelen, a few sparks could quickly spread fire through the whole settlement and destroy it entirely.

There is a small farm building, to house the camp's livestock, where there are cows, sheep, hens and ducks. It forms a little rural oasis in the midst of the general bleakness, besides providing us with fresh meat and eggs from time to time. Green vegetables are grown in the greenhouses and the kitchen garden and supply precious vitamins to our diet of tinned food. The 1955 mission had brought a few reindeer with them and a herdsman from Lapland to look after them. I hope that this experiment in acclimatization will be more successful than the attempt to introduce mules a few years ago.

I cannot forget the mournful sight of the great black mule which in 1953 was all that was left of that batch of livestock. This wretched beast had never been put to any use, in fact it had been almost abandoned, and wandered about the camp night and day, sheltering behind the huts and having to shift with every change of wind. A few people took pity on it and fed it occasionally, but mainly it had to make do with what it could find in the dustbins, showing an odd taste for munching old films. It was the living image of the island of desolation, and its fate was hotly argued between those who had a poetical attachment to this symbol of their dreams of the green pastures at home and those who had a taste for fresh meat. Naturally the butchers overcame the poets, and the mule disappeared from the scene to reappear in the form of roasts and steaks for an astonishingly long time.

In such a well-founded camp our life was obviously not at all adventurous. It was carefully organized, commonplace and comfortable, and but for the distance from our homes and friends, the difficulties of life in a closed community, the lack of distractions and especially the climate, it was very like living in a remote French village in the mountains.

When I first came to it, the base was more like a factory than a scientific station. Although the buildings looked so sound and well fitted, we soon found that there were all sorts of faults which had to be put right. The repairs were gradually organized, and the chief of each service looked after his own section. The trucks had delivered all the gear from the *Vercors*, and there was such an enormous pile of cases in front of my hospital that I wondered anxiously if we should ever get them through the doors. For more than a month Father Menu and I were busy sawing, planing and nailing planks to make shelves, going through the great stock of old medicines, many of which had gone bad, and sorting and arranging the stock we had brought with us. Nearby, Chastain, the botanist, was busy organizing his laboratory, cleaning, sweeping, knocking in nails and hunting for rats. And so it went on throughout the camp.

This work did not prevent me from going on excursions to see the country. Before going further, I must refer the reader to the maps and say a little about the geography of the island. Kerguelen is a volcanic island, and Mount Ross, its highest peak (6450 feet), is an extinct volcano now covered with eternal snow. Kerguelen is not a single small island, but a large group covering more than twenty-five hundred square miles — about as big as Corsica. The main island is eighty-five miles by seventy-five. The coast is deeply indented, like a piece of a jigsaw puzzle, with long and narrow peninsulas linked to the land by narrow necks, and fjords piercing far inland. Our base at Port-aux-Français lies at the head of the deepest fjord, Morbihan Bay. This considerable area is surrounded by a necklace of three hundred islands and islets as well as innumerable rocks, which make coastal navigation very dangerous.

The Courbet Peninsula is the best-known part of Kerguelen, because our base at Port-aux-Français lies on its southern coast. To the west it is most mountainous, with a number of peaks more than three thousand feet high. On its eastern side the peninsula slopes down rather steeply to a low, marshy plain — the only flat part of Kerguelen — which reaches to the shore and is so low that it is hardly visible from the sea.

This is the part of the island richest in wild life. Since the plain faces east and is therefore fairly sheltered from the western gales, sea elephants find it easy to land on the immense sandy beaches, where there is plenty of room for them to settle their seraglios and bring up their young. At some seasons the beaches teem with them. On the same beaches there are penguin rookeries sometimes consisting of hundreds of thousands of birds, and often with colonies of cormorants next door. In the grasslands next to the shore albatrosses and giant petrels come to nest, lay their eggs and brood. And in this nursery the fledglings grow up until they learn to fly.

This marshy land next the shore, which seethes with

animal life of every sort, is a world apart, active and alive, a strange contrast to the lonely wastes further inland. Moreover, it grows the chief and almost the only species of plant on the island, acaena grass, which fringes the sea with low-lying meadows. In summer this greenery is the only cheerful sight in this bleak land. In winter, frostbitten by the bitter wind and the snow, it turns yellow and dry until it is indistinguishable from the yellow soil and surrounding fields of gravel.

Leaving this coastal strip one comes to the stony heart of the island — sad, grim country, quite colorless and dead. This is the domain of the mountains, but they are utterly unlike our Alps or green-skirted Pyrenees, wooded, living and adorned with the delicate beauty of their plants and flowers. These mountains are cold and lusterless, as dreary as the black basalt rocks of which they are built, without flowers, green pastures or flocks. It is a world of stone, vast bare wastes of rock which help to make the island look so desolate. In the rainy season the streams, which are usually clear, break into waterfalls and rapids and sometimes swell into flood so suddenly as they approach the coast that they become quite dangerous and make it difficult if not impossible to find a way along the shore. There are chains of innumerable small lakes along the glacial valleys, and set in the moraines, these clear and shining patches have an unexpected romantic charm in the heart of this despairing landscape.

Unlike the coast which teems with life, the interior is almost dead. Here and there a strange umbelliferous plant, the azorella, covers the ground with its large spongy cushions. The botanist might also notice some lichens and mosses and a few species of grass, but they do nothing to improve the landscape. There is not a tree, not a bush, not a shrub on the whole surface of the island. The wind has seen to that. The only plant fit to eat is the famous Kerguelen cabbage, which is often mentioned by the old navigators, who found it a good tonic against scurvy. But now it is almost extinct, and is found only in the small deserted islands where there are no rabbits. On the main island these insatiable rodents have set about destroying them, and one finds only rare specimens, lodged on steep rock faces out of reach. On the way down to the coast the valleys open into treacherous morasses through which it is difficult and sometimes dangerous to walk. The gentle grasslands, so green and attractive, which are so pleasant to walk on after the hard jagged rock, now turn out to be bogs in which one sinks up to one's knees and where even the weasels' broad tracks get stuck.

Nevertheless, in spite of its austerity, the natural scenery of Kerguelen lacks neither character nor grandeur.

Fifty Men on a Desert Island

I love its severe and savage beauty, which satisfies my taste for desert spaces. The naked steppes with their rows of dry and barren hills recalled some of the lonely wastes in Mongolia and Tibet, and the huge expanses of broken stones reminded me of Oisans, the only Alpine Massif that is at all like the mountains of Kerguelen. Mount Ross is an admirable mountain. I could look at it all day. It is often veiled in cloud, but in fine weather it shakes off its shroud and stands up like a pure crystal cone against the blue of heaven. It seems quite near, although it is forty miles from Port-aux-Français. Mount Ross looks large, although it is only 6450 feet high, for it rises sharply near the coast, and its ice-clad slopes dominate the sea.

The light effects are often very beautiful, never crude, but always tempered with delicate pastel tones. The buildings at Port-aux-Français look out over Morbihan Bay, and from my window I could enjoy the sober harmony of this great dark pool with patches of seaweed on its glistening shores. In the background the volcanic cone of Mount Wyville Thomson stands out cleanly against the sky. In winter, when the bay is veiled by a curtain of mist, its snowy peak seems suspended in the sky and looks astonishingly like Fujiyama.

The scene never looks the same, and the way it changes with the weather is quite remarkable. One moment it seems peaceful, glowing in the gentle sunshine, and a few hours later it can become sinister and desolate, like a polar landscape. This peculiar variety is due to the climate, and it is time I said something on this subject.

If you look at the position of Kerguelen on the map you will see that the archipelago is situated about 49 – 50° south, which corresponds in the Northern Hemisphere to the latitude of Normandy. But the comparison means nothing. In the Northern Hemisphere the land masses are concentrated near the pole, but the great southern oceans are almost empty of land, and this makes for a totally different kind of weather. Kerguelen is very close to the antarctic convergence and exposed to the violent west winds, with their deep barometric depressions, which combine to produce a climate much more like that of Iceland or Greenland than that of Normandy.

The surrounding ocean prevents extremes of temperature, which hardly differs in summer and winter. Obviously, since it lies in the Southern Hemisphere, Kerguelen's seasons are the reverse of ours, but they have much less character than in our northern climates. Spring and autumn are quite indistinct, and the contrast between winter and summer is fairly slight. During the last three years the average temperature of the hottest month (January) was 46° F. and that of the coldest month (June) 32.2° F., with an average throughout the year of 39.5° F. The winters are never very cold. The lowest temperature registered in 1953 was 15° F. Likewise the summers are never hot, with a maximum temperature of 60° F. The sea varies between 45° F. in summer and 35° F. in winter.

But although the change in climate throughout the year is not great it may change remarkably within a short time. A difference of 18° F. in the same day is not uncommon, and often enough a sunny day suddenly becomes overcast and an icy wind begins driving down snow or sleet. Similarly in winter, one may have an hour of warm bright sunshine suddenly followed by gales and snow. These violent changes are caused by the great cyclonic zone of the southern front — the area of low pressure which lies between latitude 50° and 60° south.

Rain and snow are very frequent both in summer and winter. One can reckon on twenty wet days every month, but if days without rain are rare, so are days without sunshine. It is the monotonous inconstancy of the weather, rather than its severity, which is so unpleasant at Kerguelen. It seems to be November all the time, and the sudden changes of weather are very trying to certain temperaments. One has to endure all the inconveniences of cold weather without the pleasures which dry cold and good snow can provide. The snow in Kerguelen simply turns into slush and mud. Although snow is constantly falling, both in winter and in summer, it thaws at once and the strong wind prevents it from lying deeply. Only very rarely can one go on skis, and even then one has to take great care, because the snow is so thin and the ground so stony.

But the greatest curse of Kerguelen is the wind, which blows harder and more constantly than it does anywhere else, except perhaps in some parts of the antarctic, such as Adélie Land. In 1953 we had three hundred days of wind classified as "fresh gale," which in meteorological language indicates a speed of forty miles per hour or more, and one hundred and three days of "whole gale" — that is to say, blowing at more than fifty-five miles per hour for at least an hour at a stretch. The strongest wind in 1953 was one hundred and sixteen miles per hour, and the maximum ever recorded at Port-aux-Français one hundred and thirty miles per hour. This is extraordinary enough, but probably the wind reaches even greater speeds further inland. Naturally such ferocious winds can have a shattering effect on some people's nerves. The whole camp shudders in the storm, electric wires shriek, huts shiver down to their foundations and sand blows in everywhere. Out of doors everything takes wing, and it is a common sight to see empty packing cases or corrugated-iron sheets flying across the camp like wisps of straw. If one has the bad luck to be caught in a storm away from the camp it is a very hard job to get home. One can make only slow headway, bent double if the wind is in one's face, and leaning back and digging in one's heels for dear life it it comes from behind. Some of my companions have seen waterfalls in the mountains that streamed upwards, driven up by the rising airstreams. This may sound a tall story, but it is certainly true.

Every year in February we enjoy our chief diversion, which is also the only one of its kind: the visit of the *Tottan*, the ship going to relieve the Australian mission at Heard Island. This island lies three hundred miles south of Kerguelen and is much smaller and much bleaker in climate, since it is within the antarctic zone. The mission consists of ten Australian technicians and scientists who, like us, are relieved every year. They always call at Kerguelen on their return journey and greatly appreciate their visit, which gives them an opportunity of seeing fresh faces and enjoying the good food and better wines at Port-aux-Français in a friendly atmosphere.

On February 28 the *Tottan* was sighted in Morbihan Bay, and soon afterwards we saw her picket boat ap-

proaching the shore and went down to the landing stage
to the meet the Australians. We spent the next two days
making merry and fed our guests with banquets washed
down with the best wines from our cellars, champagne
and stronger liquors, to which the Australians did full
justice. The *Tottan* brought us also letters from France
forwarded from Australia and took away our mail with
the first photos of our life in Kerguelen. The whole
camp was in a fever of letter-writing which finished only
on March 2, when the *Tottan* put out to sea. Then we
settled down to our life of solitude, which was to last till
we were relieved in December.

After these few days of relaxation, work began again
with new energy, for we had a very full program and
the few fine days were interrupted by many days of bad
weather during which it was impossible to work out of
doors. It is true that we had plenty to do indoors, for the
inside fittings were in a bad way and almost all needed
to be repaired or replaced. The most difficult problem
in this region of perpetual wind was to make the windows airtight. Even with the best and most up-to-date
methods, it was impossible to keep out rain and dust
when they were hurled at the windows by eighty-mile-
an-hour winds. It was the same with the roofs, which
had to be entirely relaid and caulked like a ship's bottom. The overhead electric wires were constantly being

ripped down by the wind, and the only remedy was to replace them piecemeal by underground cables. All this work, to say nothing of putting in central heating, painting and mending buildings, and repairing the motor vehicles, which suffered abnormally hard wear on difficult ground, kept most of the camp busy most of the time.

There was also no lack of outside work. New Fillod huts had to be made for the soldiers and two great pylons had to be erected for the radio station. The camp was turned into a vast building site where concrete mixing went on all day long. Everyone, including the head of the mission, the administrators and the service chiefs, took a hand in the work, which had to be finished before the winter.

In this wild country the smallest job becomes an adventure. The simple task of handling cement in a high wind is a most disagreeable occupation. As for sand, one often has to go a long way to collect it, and then it is usually mixed with seaweed, so that it has to be thoroughly washed under a powerful jet of water. I remember one morning in February when the landing craft full of men and gear put out to sea towing a raft, supported by two of the engineers' boats, to fetch gravel from near Point Molloy, an hour's run from Port-aux-Français. During the short passage the wind got up suddenly and blew so hard that it began driving the raft towards the open sea, towing the landing craft, which had not a powerful enough engine to withstand the force of the wind. The only way to avoid a catastrophe was to abandon the raft, which drifted away with its cargo and soon sank. I could give many other examples, but this one should be enough to show how the vile climate of Kerguelen may transform a perfectly safe and simple piece of work into a difficult and dangerous adventure.

But fortunately none of this affected my medical work, although the dust was a great curse to me when it found its way into every corner of the operating theater, so that I had to keep sterilizing my instruments and equipment. My patients were few and the general health of the mission was excellent, apart from digestive trouble from eating too much tinned food. To make up for the deficiencies caused by this regime, I introduced a regular distribution of vitamin pills, with excellent results. The health of the mission was, moreover, controlled by a monthly medical examination of every member of the staff, whose weight and blood pressure were duly recorded.

This medical work left me a great deal of leisure, and I had all the time I needed for biological research and to make a documentary film of the wild life. I was also able to complete several studies of oriental subjects with the help of the books, manuscripts and other documents

I had brought with me from France. This threefold activity left me no time for boredom, and I felt perfectly happy in this harsh and wild country, which I was beginning to love. A solitary life among serene and splendid natural scenery suited my taste exactly. I was surrounded by pleasant companions, but I was able to get away from them and be alone in one of the deserted valleys or lonely beaches near the base, among a peaceful and friendly population of penguins or sea elephants.

From the very start I found it easy to preserve my precious solitude in the center of this community, while having daily dealings with the men I was responsible for, who came to consult me when they felt ill, overtired or depressed. They tactfully respected my solitude, knowing how much I prized it. I felt very far away from France, not only in space but in spirit, and I did not regret for a moment my decision to come to Kerguelen. I even began to recover my inner balance, which had escaped me in Paris and which I had been seeking for in vain ever since I left the Far East. I was now able to pursue the meditations which I had had to give up in France, where neither the inner nor the outer environment had allowed me to think.

Winter drew on, the days became shorter, frosts and snowfalls more frequent, and the sea elephants went away. On one occasion it snowed for eight days without stopping, but the blizzard drove the snow away before it was very deep. The temperature varied between 32° F. and 18° F. — nothing to complain of in our well-warmed dwellings. June 21 is a great holiday in all the southern missions. It is the feast of the winter solstice, which marks the halfway line in our year of exile and announces the coming of better days. We celebrated it this year with feasting and jollity — the most popular of our entertainments being, as usual, a revue in which every member of the mission received his little parcel of home truths, presented without malice. It was entitled *Adventurers in Slippers* and the theme provided a full program.

Similar festivities followed not long afterwards in honor of July 14, when we had the finest fall of snow in the whole year. It was unusual in that it fell in fairly calm weather, so that it lay thick on the ground and reached to the mountains on the distant skyline. The sun shone brightly and transformed the bleak countryside into a dazzling white fairyland. As we had among us a small detachment of engineers from the army, our national fête became a military occasion. Our soldiers paraded and the colors were saluted. Even I, who would never normally take part in such goings-on and am not particularly attracted by them, found that I was almost moved by this little ceremony, with its mixture of homeliness and heroism, in a far-off corner of French soil lost in the immensity of the southern ocean. A torch-light tattoo, an official preprandial speech and a sumptuous banquet completed the festival, and afterwards we went off skiing.

The monotony of communal meals and an almost unchanging menu were sometimes broken to celebrate birthdays and births. The births of course did not take place at Port-aux-Français, but in families at home. The flood of them during the first months was quite extraordinary, though no doubt it is easily explained by the warmth of the fathers' fond farewells. There was hardly a week in which we did not drink the health of a happy father, and once there were as many as three births in a single day. The births stopped after the month of September — at all events they were no longer celebrated. A birthday also provided an excuse for a party, and I still like to recall a birthday cake in honor of the "oldest member of the mission," a friendly tribute from my younger friends.

Winter is the great time for indoor work and for two months the hospital was at the mercy of the painters. This kept me always on the move carrying heaps of medicine bottles and boxes from one room to another. This unwelcome work was not improved by the horrible racket of the compressor outside my window and by the stench of paint from the paint spray which seeped into every corner of the building. This had to happen when one of my patients showed symptoms of acute appendicitis. I might have to operate at any moment, so I chucked the painters out of part of the hospital so that I could have the operating theater ready, and sterilized everything over again for this emergency. I was a bit anxious about operating in such unhygienic conditions, but the appendix had the tact to respond to applications of ice, so I was able to put off the operation to a more convenient time.

The persistently bad weather complicated everybody's work, especially the meteorologists'. They had to make observations at fixed times, and the simple business of walking across the camp to read their instruments, which were some distance away, was quite an ordeal. I often watched them with admiration bending to the blizzard and struggling against the wind as they went to perform their modest but indispensable duty. Even the botanist sometimes had a job, which may seem odd in a land where one can't see a plant for miles. But in fact, although the visible flora consists of only a few tufts of azorella and meadows of acaena grass which dry up in winter, there are a large number of minute plants, and very little is known of their biology and methods of adapting themselves to the climate. Chastain was making a careful study of the climate in which these plants lived. He had planted recording thermometers at a number of points some distance apart, and to go and read them all in the middle of a hurricane was no easy task. And it was much the same for most of the other scientists — the geologist and those doing research on the ionosphere.

This side of life at Kerguelen is too often forgotten. Life in the mission, I must repeat, is by no means risky or adventurous. It is not a struggle against great danger or a vicious climate, but a constant fight against petty, prosaic difficulties which make one's ordinary, everyday task painful and thankless. The work is unnoticed and inglorious, it needs much courage and will, but in the *bourgeois* comfort of the base we cannot claim the hero's halo that we might earn in other distant missions.

In winter our morale is at its lowest. It is exciting to leave France, and a new experience to sail to Kerguelen. Unloading is full of adventures, and one's new home is picturesque, with odd and interesting animals to study. But after six long months of monotonous days the adventure has lost its sparkle. The perpetual wind and fickle weather, with the barometer forever changing, have tried the nerves of many. Our daily work is tedious, and the diet monotonous; the timetable is inflexible, the camp ugly and the landscape unvarying. There are no distractions to prevent one from worrying about one's distant family. Six months of this life has changed men's characters, embittered their spirits and made them so hypersensitive that some of them can no longer bear to live together. When this state of mind is aggravated by the tactlessness, unbridled criticism and thoughtless gossip of some, and the bad temper, intolerance and lack of understanding of others, some members of the mission reach a state of strain that is apt to end in violence.

Separate closed cliques are a great cause of this strain. Men are loyal to their own clique instead of to the mission as a whole. It could be seen during the voyage, but the evil has grown since then. There is one clique of administrators, another of radio men and meteorologists, there are the scientists, and there is the largest group of all, the soldiers and workmen from the engineers. The fact that the cliques are of such different sizes makes things worse, and the scientists, who are by far the smallest group, are inevitably persecuted. A botanist's or a geologist's work is not spectacular. Unlike the engineers, they cannot produce new buildings or pylons to show for it. The value of their work will appear only much later, when the results of their studies are published. And until then the laborers turn up their noses at the scientists, whose work seems to be pointless. They are not eager to help in a task they cannot understand. The scientists depend on the carpenters to keep their laboratories working, and on the mechanics for serviceable weasels to take them on expeditions. The mechanics are not too keen on providing these vehicles for scientific expeditions, which they tend to regard as mere pleasure trips. The administration does not make these difficulties easier by preferring public works (photos of new buildings look well in official reports) to the less photogenic and less obviously interesting work of exacting scientists whose demands are never satisfied.

Moreover there is no doubt that for young men who cannot sublimate their natural instincts on a higher plane prolonged continence can seriously upset their physical and mental balance. They live in a world where their preoccupation with sex is constantly encouraged by ribald conversations, jokes, songs, pictures and the books they read. As a result there are wild incidents, at once absurd and truculent, which, in the overheated crucible of the mission, tend to assume an importance which they do not deserve. And this is rather sad.

The transition from winter to summer was desperately slow and imperceptible. There was hardly a sign of spring. But little by little nature awoke, a few green shoots were visible in the faded yellow fields of acaena and the skuas began to come back. But the real sign that spring had come to Kerguelen was the return of the sea elephants. They spend the whole winter out at sea, and come back in September to give birth to their young. I shall have much more to say about them later. The wandering albatrosses also returned and one began to meet a few of these splendid birds in the meadows, dancing the nuptial dance and building their nests.

Outdoor work began again all the more feverishly because very few months remained to complete our heavy program. The station for ionospheric research was finished and its two great pylons erected, but the biggest piece of work, the seismological station at Point Molloy, had still to be done. This was an almost superhuman task in Kerguelen's vile climate. The station is an hour by sea from Port-aux-Français, and the frequent gales make it very risky to take material there. The whole building had to be hewn out of the rock to prevent any disturbance irrelevant to the seismograph. This meant digging out and taking away hundreds of cubic yards of rock. But in spite of the appalling difficulty of this task, which kept the whole camp busy, it was finished before the relief party arrived and was in working order by the beginning of 1954. When its three sections are complete it will be the largest seismological installation in the whole Southern Hemisphere.

We also took up another task, and set about completing the triangulation and map of the central plateau which had been begun by previous missions. Exploring parties went off inland, and made three expeditions, one of which lasted more than a week, before their tour of duty was over. They brought back important observations which were sent off to the National Geographical Service. These expeditions entailed a lot of hard work, the going was very difficult, and the country quite inaccessible to any kind of vehicle, even those with caterpillar tracks, so the party had to carry everything on their backs: food, clothes, camping kit and surveying instruments.

My only regret during my year at Kerguelen was that I was not able to go on these long expeditions, which would have been a great joy to an old mountaineer. But I was responsible for the health of the mission, and I could not go away for a week when forty men were doing heavy work and might have an accident at any time or be taken suddenly ill. But I was able to make plenty of shorter excursions to places nearer to the camp, during which I kept in touch with the base by radio and could hurry back if there were an emergency call. Thus I could get on with my biological research and take a large number of photographs and documentary films of the animal life in Kerguelen.

CHAPTER THREE

Man and Solitude

AUTHORS of travel books are very fond of the easy expedient of publishing extracts from their logbook. They think it will make their story more lifelike if they invite the reader to share their lives, their adventures and their emotions day by day; and often they succeed. But if I did this with Kerguelen, I fear that I should reproduce only too painfully the ghastly monotony of our life in the mission. There is only one part of such an existence that can possibly be of interest: one's individual spiritual and intellectual life. Naturally this does not appear in the actions recorded in logbooks, and much of it is not capable of being described.

The most remarkable thing is the difference between the way different members of the mission behave, although they all live in identical conditions. It is noticeable after the first few months. Some people find the loneliness very hard to bear, especially when it is combined with a communal existence from which they cannot escape. It has a very bad effect on their character, making them unduly susceptible, and hypercritical, until they are almost impossible to live with. Others relapse into boredom and don't know what to do with themselves when their work is done.

The truth is that for most of mankind solitude is the most difficult thing to bear and also the most difficult to conceive of in its fullest sense. Solitude is a *tête-à-tête* with oneself, and that is what most men hate, for they are bored by their own selves and are afraid of meeting them. That is the cause of the reactions I have been speaking of, the worst of which is not plain boredom but vicious ill temper towards companions in misfortune. This is even worse, because it tends to destroy the real value of solitude and its only justification, which is that it prepares one for a closer communion with the Divine Being and our fellow beings.

Here I must explain what I mean about the value of solitude. When I was an active mountaineer, from 1920 to 1935, it was in the Alps that I found complete solitude among scenes of incomparable beauty and purity. Although the glaciers and easier peaks were thronged with tourists, I had only to climb for a few hours to lose all sight of them and find utter solitude and perfect peace among the silent ice and rocks which had kept their pristine purity since the beginning of the world. I was outside space and time, in a world apart, far from the vain strife of mankind. I remember expeditions that lasted several days on the Italian slopes of Mont Blanc, when we sheltered in forgotten huts where no living creature but the eagles and the choughs came to disturb us, and our little string of climbers was the only human element in a world of stone and ice. Our utter isolation made us feel that we alone possessed this splendid kingdom, as if some cataclysm had destroyed the world of men and had forgotten us in this lost fold of the mountains. This gave me a moving sense of unity: unity first with my companions, symbolized by the rope that linked us together, but far stronger and more durable. It was a true brotherhood, born on the unsullied rock with all the strength of a shared passion, and growing in this pure world where man is alone in the heart of ruthless and inhuman mountains, untroubled by any world cares. It is a strong bond, made of a hundred different strands, climbing on the mountainside or resting for the evening in a shelter or in camp, talking for hours or sitting in silence round the fire. Certainly the most precious and unchanging friendships in my life have been made on the slopes of mountains.

Then there is the sense of unity with the mountains and, through the mountains, with the universe. The hand-to-hand struggle with rock or ice can give the

Man and Solitude

climber a sense of almost physical possession, but besides this feeling, which is chiefly of triumphing over difficulty, there is sometimes a subtler feeling of taking part in the secret life of the mountains and of the world. I have felt it when climbing dangerous slopes of ice; as I forced my way through a huge fabric of crumbling seracs, I felt as if I were committing a sort of rape: an uncomfortable sense of having broken into the virgin fastness of this world of ice and sullying its unsubstantial purity with my presence.

It was on the mountains that I had my first inkling of cosmic unity, of taking a ludicrously small but real part in the forces of the universe, and this idea came to take an important place in my life. The same cosmic force that quickened my body and soul moved the sun and stars above my head and governed the rocks and glaciers beneath my feet, which at any moment might slide into an avalanche and overwhelm me in the mineral world. The same force made the torrent spring out of the heart of the glacier and sent the screaming chough whirling in the sky; it united me to my companions, and gave life to the whole world around us.

I have had this sensation even more deeply when climbing alone. I have sometimes spent a whole week alone in a hut high up on the Pyrenees, going out each day on skis and coming back each night to the lonely shelter with nothing but a wood fire to keep me company. I loved the mountains too much to be content with short holiday visits, and wanted to spend my whole life among them and know them in all their moods. This dream came true when I spent two years as a doctor to a small village five thousand feet up in the heart of Oisans.

Gradually the mountains altered my first view of solitude. I had thought of it as purely negative, the mere absence of men. I had fallen under its spell and had been tempted to think of it as an end in itself, but, although I needed it so much to escape from commonplace human contact even with those I loved, I did not see how it could help those who looked to it for guidance. Then the feeling of unity with my companions symbolized by the rope that joined us made me realize that while isolation was the first step towards freedom from worldly matters, one had no right to hide in an ivory tower absorbed only in oneself. So the mountains, to which I had first been drawn by a love of action, stimulated the contemplative part of my nature and created an inner conflict, and a desire to understand my passion for solitude and unity with the absolute. I was not content with the modest light that had been kindled in my spirit. The Cartesian doctrines which had been dinned into my head since my earliest youth would not let the problem alone, but had to probe and dissect — which was quite enough to extinguish the light completely.

As a result of all this travail I entered the Cistercian Order and spent a year in religious meditation. But I found that although the austerity and silence of this life of self-communion gave me great happiness, I was out of place there and out of harmony with its dogma and philosophy.

It was not until almost ten years later, in a little Tibetan retreat, that I really began to understand the problem I was trying to solve. My long reflections in the silent cloisters there led me to modify and enrich my first intuitive idea of solitude, casting off the negative aspects of isolation and withdrawal, which can only lead to self-absorption and sullen egotism. I now realize that solitude is much more than this: it is a means of attaining a fuller and richer life and a deeper and more real communion with other men, considering them not as strangers, nor even as brothers, but as an integral part of one's own self. And this self is no longer the narrow individual ego, but has become an element of the cosmos, one of the innumerable streams that form the universal river of life, one of the countless forms in which the absolute appears.

It also seemed to me that there was a permanent conflict between my youthful dreams of action and adventure and my deep desire for solitude and contemplation. Whenever I have tried to withdraw from the world I have been interrupted by the brutal need for action, sometimes by circumstances outside my control, but sometimes conspiring with the restless demon within me.

The problem of solitude and the inner life occurs in ordinary present-day life. Man is hardly ever alone; his life is more and more invaded by the madding crowd from which it is becoming impossible to escape. But what is more serious is that men are becoming less and less anxious to escape. I found that my companions at Kerguelen were bored when they were alone, because in their past social existence their inner life had withered away. In France a man can find a hundred ways to avoid being alone by himself: his family, friends, the movies and many others. When his work is over he can find a complete change of atmosphere in entirely different surroundings. There was nothing of the kind in Kerguelen: no movies, no family, no chance of changing his environment. His only resource is to retire into his room; but there he will find the other, the one in whose company he does not wish to be, the self from whom he longs to escape without knowing how to do so.

Man and Solitude

Many of the men had to work together, but even those of us — the scientists, the doctor and some of the technicians — who worked alone, were forced to meet at mealtimes. We met for breakfast, lunch and dinner in the great dining hall, sitting in dozens at separate tables, according to our jobs. There was a special table for the senior staff, where the head of the mission, the administrators and the principal service chiefs sat together. These artificial groups were agreeable enough to begin with. We did not know one another well, and everyone had a chance of making an impression. But soon they became irksome, and sometimes unbearable, so that some members of the mission did not come to meals at all. It would have been better to have changed places at table frequently, for however interesting a man may be, it does not take long before one knows all his stories, and one soon finds that even the most gifted man's conversational assets are very poor if one has to listen to him three times a day for a whole year. This is why no man is a hero to his family or his valet.

When one has been through all the ordinary subjects of conversation one gets to know in advance how each man will react: whether he will agree, contradict or lose his temper. Certain subjects are taboo because they are sure to provoke quarrels. And everyone has his little tricks, his own way of eating or drinking, his own jokes and gestures, his political, intellectual or artistic hobby-horses. One can enjoy these things for a couple of months, but after that they become terribly tedious. These reflections are obviously far from novel. They could have been made by anyone who has taken part in an expedition and lived for a while in a closed community, but I cannot overlook them, if I am to give a true picture of life at Kerguelen.

CHAPTER FOUR

A Living Desert

LIFE at Kerguelen is terribly dull and ordinary, the atmosphere in the mission is tedious and sometimes quite unpleasant, but there are wonderful opportunities of escape. If one cannot take refuge in one's inner self, Kerguelen is prodigal of the treasures of its wild and lonely valleys, endless beaches and, best of all, prolific animal life. When one has had enough of the camp with its futile arguments, petty scandals and jealousies, it is infinitely restful to turn to the peaceful communities of penguins and sea elephants.

Since it is a lonely piece of land in the middle of a vast ocean, Kerguelen is a natural sanctuary for wild life, and one finds restricted to quite small areas interesting animals in incredible quantities. These animals are naturally almost all marine creatures that live in cold seas. As in all cold countries, the different species are very few, but there are large numbers of individuals of each species. This is a result of their hard life and the high death rate, so that only the most successful and populous species survive.

Thin Edge of the World

All the marine animals, whether mammals, like the sea elephants and sea lions, or birds, like the penguins, petrels and albatrosses, pass most of their lives in or on the water, where they find their food. They come to the beaches of Kerguelen only at certain stages of their annual cycle, particularly at the breeding season.

The strictly land animals include a few invertebrates — insects, spiders and *acarids* — which are interesting chiefly to specialists, though it is worth noting how they adapt themselves to the climate and the strong winds. There are virtually no flying insects. There are two species of wingless fly which look like ants when one sees them crawling among the acaena shoots, and two species of butterfly which have such stunted wings that they look much more like grasshoppers than lepidoptera.

There is one land animal which plays an important part in the life of Kerguelen: the rabbit; but it is not indigenous. Rabbits were imported in 1874 by the British ship *Volage*, which marooned several pairs for the benefit of shipwrecked sailors. This was a good idea, for shipwrecks were common at this time, when whaling and seal hunting were at their height. These rabbits were no less prolific than the rest of their kind, and they have now conquered the whole island, where they continue to multiply.

It is a pleasant and homely sight to come upon them

in the acaena fields, standing with their ears pricked, like sentries before their warrens, and their little white scuts bobbing away in all directions as one approaches. Unfortunately they cause much damage. When they dig their holes in the acaena fields the wind at once carries the loose soil away, leaving bare patches in the meadows. They also nibble at the banks of azorella and gradually destroy them. It has been suggested that they should be wiped out by an artificial epidemic of myxomatosis, but the authorities decided to put up with them, because the inhabitants of Port-aux-Français enjoy rabbit shooting and are glad of a supply of fresh meat. I should add that they do not multiply as fast in Kerguelen as they do in Australia, and that vast numbers of them die in the winter; when there is snow, their warrens are apt to flood and food is short. In winter it is not uncommon to see skinny rabbits nibbling seaweed on the beaches or gnawing the wooden pegs which mark our paths through the snow till they have bitten them into pieces. Starvation paralyzes their hindquarters, and by the end of winter one often sees wretched rabbits, now no more than skin and bone, which are unable to run away and can only manage a miserable crawl.

None of the other animals on Kerguelen are ever hunted. They are quite peaceful and tame and have no fear of man. It is quite easy to go right up to them and photograph them. One can even touch them. Kerguelen must be one of the few places in the world where one can walk up to a sitting bird, pick her up out of the nest to examine the eggs and replace her without alarming her in the least. As a result one can watch all the stages of the birds' lives, from the hatching of the chicks, with extraordinary intimacy. The opportunity of making friends with wild animals is one of the greatest attractions of Kerguelen. I had never enjoyed it before except in those countries, such as India and Tibet, where human compassion is bestowed on all living creatures, even the most humble, and hunting is considered a crime; where deer, squirrels, hares, marmots and even foxes live undisturbed and unafraid among men in a friendly and touching companionship.

I made several expeditions to various parts of the island and got to know the chief species of animals that inhabit it. There are two groups which far outnumber the rest of the local fauna — sea elephants and penguins. They both have a ludicrous appearance and strange habits, and deserve to be described in detail.

There is no need to go far to see sea elephants, for there are plenty of them even on the outskirts of the camp. When one first arrives at Port-aux-Français one is astonished to find that the acaena fields between the landing stage and the camp are full of huge and clumsy seals sprawling in the grass like cows in a meadow at home. They are the sea elephants (*Mirounga leonina*). They are preposterously fat and swollen, and quite impassive. They find it hard to move on land, crawling on their bellies and pushing themselves along with their short front legs. Their broad faces are lumpish and heavy-jowled, adorned with stiff mustaches, and their large prominent round eyes are constantly rheumy and running with tears. Their dilated nostrils are half blocked-up with a thick whitish secretion, and their hide is round and ugly, its dim grayish-brown speckled, mud-stained and seamed with scars. The males have large proboscises. This may not sound very attractive, but although it is so ugly and without the least flicker of intelligence, a sea elephant's face is oddly expressive and can convey better than many more intelligent animals the simple emotions of fear, anxiety, anger or bliss. And bliss is the usual expression on their faces as they sleep wallowing in the mud or basking in the sun, which is the main business of their lives. If one approaches them, they don't trouble to move away. They just raise their great heads, open their large pink mouths and emit an unmelodious rumbling noise which sounds more like a faulty digestion than the speech of an animal.

Summer is a difficult time for sea elephants. It is the

molting season, which makes them uglier than ever, with great strips of dirty brown hide coming unstuck from their sides, and gray patches of new fur showing through the gaps. When these animals molt they become quite ill with fever and catarrh of the nose and pharynx. In this season they seldom remain on the beaches, but retire inland, just as if they were ashamed of their miserable state. They gather in twos and threes in the bogs or the wet fields, where they keep rolling over on the same spot until they have dug themselves into mudholes, where they wallow all day long. Thus they massage themselves with cool mud, which helps to rub off their old skin and abate their fever. There are wallows all round the shores of the Courbet Peninsula, but they are commonest on the east coast, which at some seasons has a vast population of sea elephants, to say nothing of penguins and albatrosses. One cannot camp near these mudholes without suffering from their appalling stench and the snorts and grunts of their inmates.

When the molt is over the sea elephants leave the shores of Kerguelen for the open sea, where they pass the winter, feeding chiefly on squids and small cephalopoda. But no one knows where they go. Our only information is purely negative: they do not migrate to other subantarctic islands. There are scientific stations at Heard, MacQuarie and New Amsterdam where for

A Living Desert

some years there has been systematic marking of sea
elephants, but no sea elephant marked in these islands
has ever been discovered in Kerguelen or vice versa. It is
also very odd that one never sees sea elephants out at sea
in the winter. However, they do not all disappear during this season, and there are always a few to be found
on the beaches, but they are only a tenth or a twentieth
of the number that congregate there in spring, which is
the real sea-elephant season in Kerguelen.

Spring starts at the beginning of September, when
these animals return to the coast after their long winter
absence. The first to return are the big bulls, who are
then in the full pride of their monstrous splendor. They
are enormous beasts, sometimes getting on for twenty
feet long and weighing two tons. With his gigantic body,
his huge swollen nose bulging above his face like the
crest of a helmet, his thick hide seamed with scars, the
sea elephant looks like some terrifying beast of the
Apocalypse, although he is actually peaceable and fights
only in the rutting season.

About a fortnight later the females arrive. They have
all been carrying their young for nearly a year and are
ready to give birth. Pregnancy has not improved their
looks by covering their unsightly faces with a strange
whitish mask. They begin to bear at once and some of
the mothers just reach the shore in time. The young are

usually born at night, so the birth is naturally difficult to observe. M. Aubert de la Rüe, who spent whole days watching groups of expectant mothers, told me that he had never witnessed a birth. I was more fortunate, and have even had the extraordinary good luck to be able to film a birth in all its stages for the first time on record. The birth of sea elephants is just like that of other mammals, but the mothers have a curious habit. When they are resting for short periods between the birth pangs, they busily sprinkle their backs with sand and pebbles, which they pick up with their short, clawed paws, as if this dry douche relieved and refreshed them. I should also note that in every case so far observed the young were born tail first. The females, as a rule, have only a single baby.

The little ones are delightful creatures. They are about two and a half feet long at birth and are covered with a silky, black, curly fleece very like astrakhan. As they lie beside their mothers, they bark like puppies and get into the most ludicrous positions, sleeping on their backs like human babies and scratching themselves gently with their long curved nails, or blissfully sucking their enormous mothers' tiny teats.

The rutting season follows very closely after the young are born. The females never remain alone or scattered at random on the beaches. As soon as they arrive, the bulls divide them up, each bull collecting a harem of fifty to a hundred females, which seems to be as many as will satisfy his physiological needs. I don't know how much the pasha's own charm affects the issue, but there is no doubt that he uses all his authority to recruit his concubines, chasing any errant female and biting her sharply to show that he is the master, and at the same time driving off any possible rivals.

While the young are being born the bull keeps a fatherly and platonic eye on his harem, contenting himself with keeping order in his fractious seraglio, who have a tiresome tendency to swim out to sea. But when the real rutting season begins it becomes a full-time occupation and is all the more lively because both the old and the young males are now tetchy and quarrelsome.

The fortunate lord of the harem is usually an old bull, called the "pasha" — "harem bull" is the sealers' name. He is very jealous of his rights and keeps his eyes skinned for interlopers on his preserves. There are plenty of them — younger bulls, not yet promoted to be pashas, whom sealers call "bachelors" or "idle" bulls. They prowl around the harems all day, hoping to steal a willing female when the pasha is not looking.

This gatecrashing has its risks, for the pasha is on the alert even if he looks as if he were fast asleep. At the slightest suspicious movement or noise he raises his head, swells his proboscis in defiance and with a roar of rage hurls himself at his rival with astonishing nimbleness for so massive a creature. Usually the bachelor surprised in *flagrante delicto* makes off hurriedly without waiting to enjoy the sweets he has stolen; he knows that it would be folly to take on the rightful lord of the harem. Only a few older bulls, impatient to qualify as future pashas, accept the challenge. The fight is savage and bloody, for sea elephants make terrible wounds with their powerful level jaws and strong canine teeth, as pointed and sharp as a boar's tusks. I have often seen them with their trunks torn off or in shreds and the blood pouring from their open wounds and staining the sea around them.

During this season there is a large population of sea elephants in Kerguelen. It would be difficult to make even an approximate census, but to judge from the estimates of several observers, it must amount to between two hundred and fifty and three hundred thousand. In some places, especially on the east coast, where the sandy beaches are easily accessible from the sea for sea elephants and penguins, they come in swarms, and there are sometimes as many as five thousand per square mile. They are so thick on the ground that it is difficult to drive a weasel through the crowd, for the sea elephants take no notice of the horn; and as there are no traffic police in Kerguelen, one has to get out and kick the beasts' rumps until they deign to move out of the way.

But their numbers soon begin to decrease, and by November the harems are broken up. The females have gone on suckling their young during the rutting season, and their milk is so rich that in a month the little ones have tripled their weight and have become as fat as dumplings — so fat that they can hardly walk. They soon lose their curly black fleece, but after the first molt they have a nice new soft, silky gray coat. Now they are weaned, and their mothers leave them and swim out to sea to find food after their long and uncomfortable stay on land, during which they have eaten nothing, in spite of all that they have gone through. The young ones then migrate from the beach into the adjoining fields, where they have nothing to eat, and soon become slim and nimble enough to take to the water in their turn. But they are not away from the island for long, because in December the females and the young ones return to Kerguelen for the molt. And so the cycle closes.

Penguins are better swimmers than any other birds and move through the water like lightning. They are also very sociable and are always to be found in company. They come on land to lay their eggs, hatch them out and bring up their chicks. They breed in enormous "rookeries," but are constantly returning to the sea to catch food for themselves and their young. It consists mainly of fish, molluscs and crustaceans. They are as clumsy on land as they are speedy and agile in the water; sometimes they trip over pebbles, sometimes they waddle majestically upright or make little lurching jumps from rock to rock. If you alarm them, they throw themselves flat on their bellies and skid along on their breasts, which are covered with short thick feathers as slippery as skis, as they row themselves along with the quills on the ends of their stumpy wings. It is an odd but rapid sort of tobogganing.

There are four species of penguins in Kerguelen, and the most remarkable is the king penguin (*Aptenodytes patagonica*). It is more than two and a half feet high and is the largest of the penguins, except for the emperor penguin, which is found only on the coasts of the Antarctic Continent. Like its lesser relations, the king penguin has a black back and a broad white breast, but it has two distinctive large orange patches, shaped like inverted pears, on its cheeks. Its deportment is slow and stately, and it waddles with a regal gait, its head held high, its beak turned up and its chest puffed out, as if it were fully aware of its royal dignity. In summer one comes upon a few king penguins along the coast or in the flat coastal plain, but they are only single birds or small groups which have left their rookeries to molt in peace. To see them in their real home and to study their social behavior one must go to the east coast of the Courbet Peninsula near Cape Ratmanoff, where there are two large rookeries containing more than fifty thousand.

I have made several visits to the east coast, and have always enjoyed its beautiful scenery. It is a long day's march from Port-aux-Français, and since one has to carry a good deal of gear, what with food and sleeping bags and cameras, it is better to go by weasel. At first the route runs across the monotonous gravel fields and marshes of the lower isthmus. After that one has to cross three large streams which flow into Norwegian Bay, a lovely curved bight of shallow water, with a little island in the middle which is overgrown with azorella and looks astonishingly bright and green and makes a pleasant contrast to the drab gray all around. After leaving Norwegian Bay one heads northeast between the sea and Mount Bungay, a little hill which, although it is only two hundred and twenty feet high, stands out from the flat and dreary plain. Then one has to pick one's way through a maze of pools and marshes where it is very easy to get lost. One reaches the coast again near Charlotte Point, and after that the country becomes quite lovely. An immense stretch of fine white sand, beaten flat by the great ocean rollers, extends along the whole length of this eastern coast. It is from this beach and the north of the Courbet Peninsula only that one can get a sense of the sea's immensity, for Morbihan Bay is too landlocked ever to give such a view.

A weasel has a clear run across this splendid smooth beach, and one could drive at top speed if one did not want to keep stopping to look at interesting sights. This eastern coast is a zoological garden in which all the animals of Kerguelen are represented in large numbers. It is here that the great harems of sea elephants take up their quarters in spring. In summer the acaena grasslands next the shore are spattered with gay splashes of white — albatrosses performing their strange nuptial dances, broody females and, later, chicks — interspersed with brown patches of giant petrels, skuas and many other birds. And it is here that the king penguins and the gentoo penguins have built their great rookeries, which are what we have come to see.

I know of nothing more fascinating than to watch these rookeries of king penguins, and I spent many days among these attractive birds, camping near the rookery. As one drives along the smooth sandy beach, crowded with sea elephants basking in the sunshine, one comes upon small groups of king penguins, often with gentoos, which have wandered away from the great rookery. The birds get thicker on the ground as one approaches the colony, which is a quite remarkable sight. The whole area is littered with penguins pottering peacefully about in little bunches or waddling in Indian file. From a distance these upright bipeds in their black-and-white uniforms look extraordinarily like a crowd of human beings as tightly packed as the fashionable sunbathers on the beach at Juan-les-Pins.

I shall always remember my first morning in the penguin rookery at Cape Ratmanoff. We had pitched our camp a little way off, near a quiet and pleasant tarn. When I crawled out of my tent in the early morning I was surprised to find myself face to face, or rather nose to beak, with two splendid king penguins, who were standing just outside the door and looked as if they were wondering what could possibly live in such an extraordinary dwelling. They did not seem in the least put out by my appearing so unexpectedly, but gravely looked me up and down with dignified curiosity and did not take to their heels when I approached, but just moved off enough to keep a proper distance from me. Nearby, several others were standing in the tarn taking their morning bath, their regal figures reflected in the still water against a handsome background of hills which glowed pink in the morning sun. It was a very beautiful picture, a vision of peace in a Garden of Eden, where all was quiet and harmonious and nature was still asleep.

The whole beach, the shores of the tarn and the grass-lands stretching inland were covered with thick clusters of birds chattering together in little Parliaments of Fowls or marching solemnly behind their leaders in single file to and from the sea. Their movements seemed to be quite deliberate. They behaved as if they knew exactly what they were doing, conversing like human beings, stopping to wait for one another, starting off again and changing their course, not by chance, but with a fixed purpose. This huge population of seemingly rational and well-behaved citizens appeared to live in a perfectly organized society — which unfortunately we do not understand.

Curiosity seems to be their chief passion. While I was walking, they seemed a little worried by my size, but when I stopped and sat down, they came up slowly and cautiously, a few steps at a time, stopping to talk the matter over, and then moving a little nearer, until in the end they were only an arm's length away in an admiring circle of upright little figures in elegant and spotless white shirt fronts. But their friendly curiosity was al-ways reserved and they never took any liberties. When I stretched out a hand, they retreated modestly, maintaining their dignity and taking care always to be circumspect and a little distant.

But in spite of their gravity they are jolly creatures with a good deal of probably unconscious humor. When they go fishing in the sea they play all sorts of games among the waves, diving under the rollers like happy children and flapping their little wings in the foam. As they return from their bath, stumbling along on their short legs, sinking into the wet sand, falling down and using their wings to hoist themselves onto their feet again, they are a very comic sight. Young sea elephants often come and sleep on the beach in the middle of one of their meetings. The penguins stare at them disdainfully and walk round with disapproving looks. When these good-humored monsters make a timid move in their direction, the penguins retreat with an innocent pretense of self-defense, and finally march away with the same imperturbable calm and a regal air of offended dignity.

The center of the rookery is the most interesting part. It is hard to understand why the penguins have chosen such a dreary place in which to hatch their eggs and bring up their chicks. It is all pebbles and muddy sand, which has been so littered with the birds' droppings mixed with loose feathers, down, shattered eggs, and the parched corpses of dead chicks, that it has turned into a stinking slough.

To understand the king penguins' annual cycle one must visit their beaches in different seasons. At about Christmas time they begin to lay. The female penguin makes no nest, but lays her egg and sits on it where it lies, even if it is surrounded by pebbles, and does not bother to push aside the pebbles or take any care to protect her single egg, which is like a goose egg, only larger. The hens sit in a very odd position. Instead of squatting on the egg like most birds, they stand up straight and hold the egg on their two webbed feet, held close together, and cover it with a broad fold of their bellies. This allows them to waddle away to a new position if necessary and carry their egg with them. They sit close together side by side, and so take up very little room, but they defend this small territory hotly with their beaks and wings. The constant traffic of penguins on the way to and from the fishing ground often disturbs the crowd of mother birds, and there are constant skirmishes, each sitting hen defending her own egg, and carrying it off to safety if she loses the fight. The birds advertise their squabbles with angry and piercing squawks which fill the whole rookery and make it quite impossible to sleep if one is camping nearby.

There are accidents during these domestic battles.

A Living Desert

Sitting hens are constantly losing their eggs, and it is an odd fact that once the mother is more than about a foot from her egg she seems quite unable to find it again. Whether this is due to lack of maternal instinct or bad sight I cannot say. Perhaps penguins' eyes are suited to vision underwater, and this may be why they blunder on land. Sometimes a neighboring penguin adopts the lost egg and broods over it, while the legitimate parent shows no signs of wanting it back. These birds make the silliest mistakes; for instance there is the old trick of substituting a snowball for their egg. They sit dutifully on the melting snow and seem quite astonished to see it getting smaller and smaller until it disappears altogether.

Mislaid or broken eggs are not wasted. Among the penguins in every rookery there are a number of white birds as big as pigeons; they are sheathbills and are found only in the Southern Hemisphere. They are busy, inquisitive and greedy, and they dart nimbly about among the clumsy penguins. As soon as an egg is broken they arrive in a flash to swallow it up. They live in a sort of symbiosis with the penguins, who put up with them meekly, and give them only a mild peck when they come too near. The sheathbills miss nothing, and if a newborn chick is hurt or lost by its mother he is quickly picked up by these indefatigable scavengers.

Thin Edge of the World

When the eggs are hatched out the rookery is arranged in its own peculiar fashion. The young birds, which are quite unlike their parents, with their thick fleece of chestnut down, are collected in the middle of the colony in a huge nursery, so crowded and so vast that it seems to undulate like a brown sea. It is entirely surrounded by an army of full-grown birds, who watch over the chicks, protecting and feeding them.

By the middle of November the young birds are almost as big as the adults. Then they molt and exchange their drab brown down for a bright new suit exactly like their parents' livery. The molt lasts several weeks, during which the down gradually falls off in large lopsided tufts at random all over their bodies. The neck usually molts last, and young penguins in smart new black-and-white plumage with a scruffy dingy brown ruff round their necks look quite indescribably odd. All through the molt one often sees them standing up on their spurs like young cocks, and constantly shaking their small wings in a quick flutter, so that the down flies off in clouds.

The gentoo penguins live in colonies very close to the king penguins, and as one drives along the beach one often sees peaceful groups of the two species living together on very good terms.

A Living Desert

The gentoo penguin (*Pygoscelis papua*) is closely re-
lated to the Adélie penguin found in the antarctic, and
is smaller than the king penguin. It has the same black
jacket and white shirt front as all penguins, but instead
of the king penguin's handsome orange patches it has a
white face and a few white feathers on the nape of its
neck. Its feet are light yellow, sometimes tinged with
pink. It is more timid than the king penguin and is
difficult to approach. If one tries to do so it dashes off in
crazy flight, stumbling over every pebble and falling
into every hole, like an old comedian of the silent
screen.

The gentoos do not stick to such fixed sites as the king
penguins, and their rookeries rarely contain more than a
few hundred birds. They move their quarters at the
slightest threat of danger, which is very easy to do because they make their homes at random, often in the
middle of pebbly beaches.

They prefer to breed in the sloping grasslands, and it
is a strange sight to see terraces of sitting hens on the
hillside. Their nests consist of little mounds of earth in
the middle of a sort of white star made of the droppings
of the sitting birds, which are very clean creatures and
prefer to keep their mess outside their own nests. They
also like to nest on the top of the enormous grassy tussocks which are so common along the east coast. Unlike

king penguins, gentoos sit right down over their eggs and brood on them like other birds. They lay two eggs and incubation lasts about six weeks.

Gentoos are very sociable creatures and they often take turns at sitting. While the male (or the female) sits on the egg, his mate stands beside the nest to keep him company. I have sometimes watched their peculiar habits. From time to time the bird beside the nest slips away surreptitiously, as if it did not want its mate to know it was going, and waddles down to the sea, picking up various companions on the way. When they reach the water's edge they all dive in at once and go fishing. A little later they march back to the rookery with full paunches. Each bird pauses for a moment beside its nest, and then after a lively confabulation it takes over the nest and its mate climbs down and goes fishing in its turn.

One must go to a different part of the island to see rock hopper penguins. Their largest rookery is at Cape Kidder, five or six hours' walk to the southwest of Port-aux-Français. I had plenty of opportunites to visit this colony, which is near Molloy Point, where the seismological station was being constructed. One can go there by sea, but the route along the shore is very beautiful and interesting.

A Living Desert

The track runs along the edge of a plateau of acaena grass from which rocky cliffs fall steeply to the sea. Occasionally it winds down to make its way across an intricate series of inlets or to run along the fine sandy beaches which in spring are covered with sea elephants. The chief obstacles are a couple of torrents which become impassable after a few hours of heavy rain. It is no treat to wade through ice-cold water halfway up one's thighs, but the variety of wild life and the beautiful landscape soon make one forget such petty inconveniences.

I shall always remember my first visit to Molloy Point, for that day — it was February 22 — was probably the finest day of the whole year. The light was wonderful, and the air was so extraordinarily clear that one could pick out the smallest details in the landscape: the deep blue of Morbihan Bay, the line of gray-green islands strung out across it like a squadron at anchor, the bastions of Mount Werth and Mount Crozier with their somber basalt rocks tinted a delicate mauve in the sun, and in the background the impressive ice-clad mass of Mount Ross, outlined against the pure blue sky and looking remarkably close.

At Molloy Point a little hut had been built where one could sleep, and there was a cooker and some emergency rations. From there an hour's walk over a stony little ridge took us to a great sandy bay from which one can easily reach Cape Kidder, a high and precipitous cliff. At the foot of this cliff the rock hoppers have built their rookery in a wilderness of fallen rocks.

The rock hopper (*Eudyptes cristatus*) is the smallest of the penguins but not the least interesting. It is not so calm as the king penguin nor so nimble-footed as the gentoo. It moves in short leaps, hopping from rock to rock, as its name implies. Like all penguins it has a black back and a white front, but its head is quite distinctive. Its beak is red, short and broad with two rows of long black and yellow plumes, beginning at the beak and running down on either side of the neck. Long black eyebrows complete its clownish make-up and give it an odd, impish expression.

Rock hoppers seem to have an unusual affection for their mates. Couples seldom separate while their eggs are incubating, and you see the male bird pressed tenderly up against his mate. The chicks are covered with a dirty black-and-white down, but when they molt their down comes off in great tufts and their plumes begin to appear quite lopsidedly, so that they look very ludicrous.

There is one other kind of penguin, the macaroni, which lives on the north coast of Kerguelen. I shall be describing this area and its fauna later.

A Living Desert

There are several kinds of albatrosses in Kerguelen, but the most handsome is the wandering albatross (*Diomedea exulans*). This splendid bird is spotlessly white, except for its black wingtips. With its haughty grace and noble bearing it is the undisputed king of the southern seas. Its wings are almost ten feet across and give it an extraordinary ability to glide and soar, which one cannot help admiring as it follows the ship, circling back and forth with infinite ease, and impudently regardless of gravity, as it dives and climbs and turns in great curves, all without once moving its wings.

Towards the end of November the albatrosses come to Kerguelen to nest. They like the acaena fields that fringe Morbihan Bay, and the beaches along the lovely east coast, where they have sea elephants and king penguins for neighbors. Unlike these creatures, they do not breed on the beach itself, but in the grasslands just inshore, and the scattered white patches of nesting females seem to bring life and light to the dark grass from the wide ocean skies. Although these great birds are so light and airy in flight, their size and weight make them awkward on land.

Before the albatrosses mate they go through a strange nuptial dance, but I did not see it until much later, and will describe it when I come to it. The female bird lays a single enormous egg in a nest raised above the ground and built of mud and acaena shoots. She looks quite magnificent as she sits in her high nest. If one comes near, she does not move away, but looks at one sideways out of a lovely clear eye, and hardly seems at all nervous. She is so tame that one can lift her up quite easily (apart from her weight and size) and look at the egg in her nest. But one must make sure to hold her beak shut, for it is very sharp and quite strong enough to cut off a finger. When one puts her back in her nest she just goes on sitting, quite calm and dignified, and merely gives a few snaps of her beak to show her disapproval.

Incubation takes a long time. The newly hatched chicks are delightful balls of pure white down with attractive yellow beaks and bright little black eyes. They grow very quickly and are fed by their parents, who keep bringing them beakfuls of food. They stay in the nest for ten months before they can fly — ten months of continual molt. It starts in the winter, the fine white down falls off gradually and a grayish-brown plumage appears underneath in patches separated by loose tufts of old down. It is only when this molt is quite finished and they are nine months old that they start learning to fly, which often takes them another month. Their plumage is now dark brown with some whitish patches on the face, the throat and the underside of the wings. During the following year their plumage becomes more and

A Living Desert

more like that of the adult birds, but they still have black marks under their wings. It takes them several years to acquire the spotless white plumage which they will wear as their wedding dress.

Giant petrels are often found in the same fields as the albatrosses, especially on the east coast of the Courbet Peninsula. The giant petrel (*Macronectes giganteus*) is a little smaller than the albatross, and is similarly powerful and majestic in flight, but it has none of the beauty and nobility. Its grayish-brown plumage, its enormous beak of no particular color, but often stained with blood, its shifty pale greenish-gray eyes, its long thin feet make it an ugly and repellent sight on land. This is not the lovely white bird which flashes out of the storm clouds and follows the ship for mile after mile, skimming round with an almost ethereal grace, bringing sailors news of distant lands and flying effortlessly across the great southern ocean, but a common scavenger. It lives on nothing but dead meat, rarely goes far from the shore over which it flies tirelessly in search of its prey, spreading around it a stench of corruption which has given it the name of "stinking petrel."

Like the albatrosses, the petrels come on land to lay their eggs; but instead of scattering they huddle together in a few particular areas in the grass meadows and on the cliffs above the sea. Their nests are very primitive and consist merely of small hollows in the earth casually lined with a few blades of dry grass. They are much more shy than albatrosses, and it is hard to get near them even when they are sitting. The female lays a single egg, and the chicks are hatched in November after two months' incubation. The young ones begin as balls of dirty-gray down and grow very quickly; meanwhile their plumage darkens till it becomes almost black. These young petrels have a very nasty habit. If you go near them they spew the contents of their stomach in a jet of thick, oily, reddish and nauseating liquid at your face. If it falls on your clothes you will never get rid of its penetrating stench.

There are large numbers of cormorants all round the coast of Kerguelen, chiefly on the rocks that look down over the sea. In some places where the long beaches are split up by small outcrops of rock one usually sees a colony of cormorants on the rocks between two rookeries of king penguins on the sands below them. On land the cormorant looks a little like a penguin, with its upright body resting on short legs, its raven-black back, broad white breast and yellow wattle at the base of the beak.

They fly very fast with rapid hectic wing beats, most

unlike the albatross's wonderful planing flight. Their take-off is especially clumsy; usually they flop off the rocks and begin to fly only when they reach the level of the sea; there they taxi heavily for a long way, like flying boats, before they are able to rise off the water in slowly ascending flight.

There are plenty of cormorants all along the coasts, but usually one sees small groups of adult birds in a fishing party. There are comparatively few nurseries, and it was only during my last excursion to the Courbet Peninsula that I was able to observe them. I shall describe them in a later chapter.

These are the chief and the most typical species on the island. There are many others which would interest only specialists, and as this book is not a zoological treatise, I shall therefore mention only a few that are occasionally met on expeditions and may be of interest.

Although the sea elephant is by far the commonest of the seals in Kerguelen, one sometimes has the luck to come upon two other interesting species, particularly the otary (*Arctocephalus gazella*), the eared or fur seal. This congenial animal used to be very common in Kerguelen, but was almost killed off by the sealers and is now very rare. It is much smaller than the sea elephant and much more lively and intelligent. Its fur is a clear fawn, quite unlike the sea elephant's spotted and seamed hide. As its name implies, it has external ears; and its hind paws, instead of being stunted little fins that are useless on land, are large enough for it to run about the ground and jump nimbly from rock to rock.

Another kind of seal is occasionally found on the coast: the sea-leopard (*Hydrurga leptonyx*). It is a real wild beast with its leopard's spots, long slim body, powerful jaws and savage teeth. It is the terror of penguins and even of young sea elephants.

I have already said a little about the sheathbills. These birds live in all the rookeries: not only those of the king penguins, but also the other penguins and the cormorants. I have often watched them in the rock hoppers' nursery at Cape Kidder, where their peculiar behavior shows real intelligence. They generally work in pairs. One of them goes and annoys a sitting female till she is so provoked that she leaves her nest to chase her persecutor away. The second sheathbill immediately pounces on the egg, spears it with its hooked beak and carries it away to eat it at leisure. They are very tame and inquisitive birds. If you stand still, they come up so close to stare at you that it is fairly easy to catch them in your hand by tempting them with a piece of bread or some other bait.

A Living Desert

The skua (*Catharacta skua*) is Kerguelen's bird of prey. It is a dark brown bird about as big as a large crow; it preys largely on small birds, which it tries to surprise in their nests, and it also hunts young rabbits. It hovers patiently above rabbit holes, and as soon as it sees a young rabbit hesitate at the entrance it dives like a plummet and splits the rabbit's skull with its beak and carries it off. Sometimes it attacks full-grown rabbits, but usually only when they are wounded or diseased.

People sometimes say that skuas are savage birds that will attack a man. They have acquired this reputation from their alarming habit of diving almost vertically at you and brushing your head with their knuckles. I admit that this feels rather shattering when it happens, but I still think that it is partly due to curiosity and that the skua intends to alarm the intruder rather than to hurt him. The popular dislike of skuas is due more to an instinctive aversion to carrion-eaters than to any real evidence. All the same, I would not put it past them to attack a single, wounded man who was unable to defend himself.

Lastly there are two kinds of birds whose neat and attractive white shapes can always be seen on the beaches, the gulls and the terns. The dominican gull

(*Larus dominicanus*), so called because of its black-and-white plumage, is very like our greater black-backed gull. It is a resident and stays on the coast all the year round. The great flocks speckle the yellow sands with black-and-white spots, and wheel into the air at one's approach with a noise of wings and harsh shrieks which sound like a badly oiled pulley.

These gulls feed on small molluscs, limpets and the huge mussels which cover the rocks in Kerguelen. In order to open these large shells they drop them onto the rocks from a great height. This explains the masses of broken shells which one finds among outcrops of rock sometimes a long way from the sea. It has also given some journalists a chance to describe Kerguelen as "the country where mussels fall from the sky."

The terns (*Sterna virgata* and *vittata*) are quite the most delightful birds on the island. They are only a little larger than swallows, and are much the same shape, being very pretty and elegant birds with their pearl-gray back and wings, white belly, long forked tapering tail, bright red legs and beak and little black cap. Their flight is graceful and it is a real joy to watch them hovering over the water almost motionless, but vibrating their slender wings very fast, and then shooting down like an arrow to pick up their minute quarry from the water. They are very courageous and full of

fight, although they are so small, and they band together to hold their own against the much larger skua.
If you accidentally go too near their nests they fly
straight at you and peck your face with their little
pointed beaks.

CHAPTER FIVE

Prelude to a New Adventure

IN October 1953 I had been in Kerguelen for ten
months, and I had found this period of exile so interesting and so valuable to my mind and spirit that I was
sad to think that my year's duty, which had passed so
quickly, would soon be ended. I was probably the only
man on the island who felt as I did, and I hardly dared
mention it to the other members of the party, who were
joyfully counting the days till they sailed and would
never have believed it was possible.

We already knew that our relief ship, the *Saint-
Marcouf* — a big Messageries Maritimes liberty ship —
was due to leave Marseilles at the end of the month and
to arrive at Port-aux-Français in the second half of
December. Like everyone else I looked forward to seeing
my family and my old friends again, but after so many
years of peace and solitude in Tibet, China and now in
Kerguelen, I rather dreaded returning to so-called nor-

mal life in the hectic and noisy Western world, where I now felt a stranger. But then I had always felt a little out of place in Europe. There was no point in worrying about the future, which still seemed very remote, so I set about packing my trunks like everyone else.

But one morning the gods of adventure took pity on me. Pierre Sicaud, the director of our mission, told me that an Australian expedition was going to call at Kerguelen in January 1954 on its way to establish a scientific base in the antarctic. The Australian mission at Heard Island was on very good terms with our own, we had often worked together on scientific and technical problems, and the two chiefs were close friends. Dr. Philip Law, Director of the Australian National Antarctic Research Expedition, had therefore invited M. Sicaud to go with them as French observer, but he had been unable to accept for private reasons. The post had been offered to two other members of our mission, but they had declined, and it was still vacant. I at once volunteered, but my name had to be submitted both to the Australian Government and the French Overseas Ministry.

Thus for several weeks I waited anxiously, wavering between hope and gloom, while these two authorities made up their minds. This unexpected opportunity meant far more to me than the chance of a wonderful journey. It had a sentimental appeal from the past and seemed an almost miraculous fulfillment of an old dream of my youth — my long-distant hopes of going to the antarctic with Captain Charcot's expedition, which had been shattered by the outbreak of war.

In spite of all my journeys to different parts of the world and the powerful attraction which Asia now held for my mind and spirit, my old dream of the antarctic still slept in the depths of my heart. This unexpected invitation at the end of a long stay in Kerguelen, when I was not at all looking forward to returning to France, was certainly providential. It was an opportunity to take my experiences on Kerguelen a stage further. There would be more action, but no lack of food for the mind, and I might hope to balance the active and contemplative tendencies of my nature and to realize at last in new solitude the unity which I had sought in all my journeys of the body and spirit.

By November everything had been arranged. Official messages had been buzzing by radio between Kerguelen, the Department of External Affairs at Melbourne and the Overseas Ministry in Paris; and now I was nominated to accompany the Australians and represent the Minister and the Department for Southern Territories. Another Frenchman, Georges Schwartz, was also to join the expedition. He had already left

France on the *Saint-Marcouf* and would arrive at Kerguelen at the end of December with the relief party. We should then both have to wait until the *Kista Dan* came. This Danish ship chartered by the Australians was due to call at Port-aux-Français about January 20, 1954.

My last few weeks in Kerguelen passed like a flash. I had plenty to do getting my polar equipment together, arranging my return passage and sorting out my luggage. I obviously could not go off to the antarctic with six cases of books, Tibetan manuscripts, notes and records. Most of them would be shipped home on the relief vessel, and I would take nothing I did not actually need. But that came to a pretty large load, for there was always the risk that the ship might be caught in the ice, so I took enough clothes and books to keep me going through a possible winter in the antarctic.

On the morning of December 14, 1953, the *Saint-Marcouf* arrived and began unloading at once in favorable weather. This was naturally a very red-letter day for the rest of my party, who were going home to France and had been living in a fever of last-minute preparations.

But I was not going with them and had to wait until the Australian expedition arrived before setting out in the opposite direction, so I was interested only in my enormous batch of letters, and in getting to know the members of the new mission, with whom I would have to live for another month.

This is certainly the most lively period of the whole year on Kerguelen, as well as being the most interesting psychologically. It seems very different according to whether one belongs to the new or the old party. Now that our year in the mission was over I saw that it had followed the usual pattern and was neither better nor worse than past and, presumably, future years. The only visible difference between us and our predecessors was that instead of leonine manes and flowing beards we had shaven heads — a fashion which I confess I began. The personal antipathies that we had contracted in the course of the year did not always take the same form as in the previous team, but they were garnished with equally crazy and preposterous grievances. No mission can escape this law, and though our successors seemed as confident as we had been when we landed, I gather that the process goes on as usual.

Although this situation fascinated me, and tempted me to analyze and understand it, I was for the moment much more interested in meeting Georges Schwartz, who was to go with me to the antarctic, and hearing his news about the Australian expedition. I immediately took to Georges and found him an ideal companion. We soon became good friends and I was very glad to be going on this voyage with him, especially as we would be the only Frenchmen on board.

Georges was a choreographer, extremely gifted and with every promise of a brilliant artistic future, who had conceived a strange passion for polar exploration, and had become extremely good at it. He had gone on Paul-Emile Victor's French polar expeditions, with which he had visited Greenland and passed two successive winters in Adélie Land: and now he was preparing to spend a third year in the antarctic, with the Australians. He is a useful man to have on an expedition, for he has specialized in huskies and sled driving. And on the Australian expedition he was also to be the oceanographer. Having lived for several years far from civilization, this sensitive and cultivated man has transferred his affections to his dogs. He loves them like his dearest friends, and in his cabin there are photographs of his favorites where one would expect to see pin-up girls. He speaks of them as tenderly and with as much understanding as if they were human beings, and to all appearances they take the chief place in his life.

Schwartz brought me fresh news about the Australian expedition. Apparently we were not going to land in Enderby Land, as I had thought, but in Mac-Robertson Land in the Australian Sector, somewhere about longitude 63° east. He told me that our ship, the *Kista Dan*, was a very fine Danish cargo boat specially constructed for navigating in ice, and that her skipper, Captain Petersen, was an expert in this difficult art. Two Royal Australian Air Force airplanes would be on board, for reconnoitering a passage through pack ice. Georges showed me the aerial photos taken by Admiral Byrd's Expedition "High Jump" in 1947, from which the Australians had spotted some rocky outcrops on the coast which might be a suitable site for their base.

He had a further piece of news which increased my enthusiasm, for it was far better than I expected. I learned that when we had finished setting up the base at Mac-Robertson Land, and had deposited the winter party of ten men, including Georges Schwartz, the ship was to sail east along the coast of Mac-Robertson Land, exploring the land by air, and if possible landing on the western shore of MacKenzie Sea. After reconnoitering Cape Amery and Sandefjord Bay, the *Kista Dan* would head for the Ingrid Christensen coast in Princess Elizabeth Land, and we should make another landing. When we had done our scientific and geodetic work there we should return to Kerguelen and Heard Island and then hurry home to Australia. All this should be enough to satisfy my taste for adventure and the antarctic. It was not without risks, the least of which was having to spend

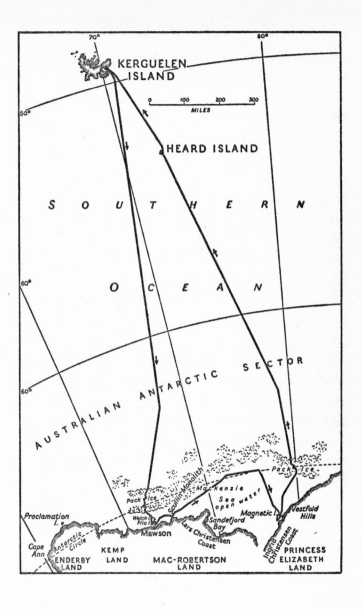

the winter in the ice. This did not depress me, in spite of the greater dangers it might involve. As it turned out our voyage was far from easy, but it was well worth our trouble.

While I was waiting for my old antarctic dream to come true, life in Kerguelen was in the topsy-turvy state that seems inevitable during the change-over. Port-aux-Français had to find food and room for twice the usual number of men. But everybody endured the overcrowding and disorganization quite good-humoredly. I was hardly affected, for there was plenty of room in my little hospital for Dr. Millet, my successor, Father Jolissaint, the new chaplain-cum-medical orderly, Georges Schwartz and myself, not to mention occasional guests. We were a happy little crew, and we spent many enjoyable evenings round the phonograph listening to long-playing records brought by the new mission.

It was a great relief and a new pleasure to be able to relax and talk to new friends with whom I had not spent a whole year. Of course they were really just the same as the people in the old mission; there were as many interesting and congenial characters in each team, at least to start with. But my new friends had the immense advantage of being new; I did not yet know their virtues and vices, their stories and their hobbyhorses, the way they thought, how they would answer particular ques-

Prelude to a New Adventure

tions or tackle particular problems — but I knew all
these things about my friends in the old mission and
they knew them about me, so that in the end we had
nothing to say to one another. With my new friends all
sorts of stale subjects suddenly seemed to come alive
again, just because someone new was talking about
them, and I found that I myself saw them from a new
point of view. In this strange way one's mind is en-
riched by a change of human air.

I had plenty to do, for while everyone was working
hard there were constant small injuries to be treated.
Moreover, the zoo at Vincennes had asked us to take
home some specimens from Kerguelen, and I had already collected several king penguins from the large
rookery on the east coast and parked them in a pen at
the base. They could not feed themselves in captivity
without help, so Georges and I had to stuff them with
scraps of fish. This was quite an awkward job, for they
are large and remarkably strong creatures. We also had
to catch a certain number of gentoo penguins and four
young sea elephants. Transporting them on the *Saint-
Marcouf* was a task worthy of Noah, but in spite of all
that could be done, and although the zoo sent an airplane to pick them up at Tamatave and fly them to
France, only the sea elephants reached France alive,
where they are flourishing and are a great success with

[115]

the public. The poor penguins, being accustomed only to the bleak climate of Kerguelen and also very difficult to feed in captivity, did not survive the passage through the tropics. They ought to have had a special chilled tank on the *Saint-Marcouf*, but it had not been foreseen when the ship left France, and we could not make one in Kerguelen.

The *Saint-Marcouf* was unloaded and loaded in record time — less than a week — and weighed anchor on Christmas Eve and headed for New Amsterdam on her way to Tamatave. I was not sorry to see her leave, for I felt that I had long ago said good-by to the 1953 mission, and to France, where they were going. I had already set out on a new adventure, which occupied all my thoughts.

I had still to wait a month in Kerguelen until the Australians arrived. I handed over my duties to Dr. Millet and was at last free of all the medical responsibilities, which for the past year had prevented me from going on long excursions on the island. I now had a chance to do so with Georges Schwartz. But nothing is easy in Kerguelen. The fickle climate and difficult terrain make any long journey from the camp into a proper expedition, and one has to find a means of transporting heavy camping gear, to say nothing of the cameras and movie cameras. We therefore had to have a weasel and its driver, but at that time they were all occupied in station duties. So, in the meanwhile, we set out, lightly equipped, to cross the sharp shoulders of Castle Mountain, from the top of which we had a very wide view of the north coast of the island, and I was able to see whether it was possible to return by weasel from Accessible Bay to Port-aux-Français.

As soon as we returned I managed to bring off what I had been projecting for so long: an expedition right round the Courbet Peninsula, in order to study the huge colonies of penguins, which are by far the largest on the island. At first we followed the usual route to the east coast, by way of the lakes of the Lower Isthmus, Mount Bungay, which we climbed, and the head of Norwegian Bay. I still found the same peculiar pleasure and fascination in the splendid sandy beaches of this beautiful coast, on which the great ocean rollers are forever beating. It is the only coast on the island which gives one a sense of the freedom and infinity of the sea.

There were still plenty of sea elephants, but not so many as in the spring, when the females give birth and the beaches swarm with harems of adults and their young families. The old bulls had almost all gone, but the young females, who had weaned their young and taken to the sea to break their long fast, were coming back on land to molt, soon to be followed by the young males. Their molting wallows were particularly thick on the boggy ground near the second of the two huts built in 1931 by sealers from the *Austral*. The hut was completely in ruins, and was so surrounded by stinking wallows with their noisy and squalid tenants that we certainly had not the least desire to take shelter there.

We came upon large flocks of king penguins, often mingled with smaller groups of gentoos, a sign that we were approaching the great rookery at Cape Ratmanoff, one of the largest in the island, with a population of nearly fifty thousand king penguins. We found some adult birds finishing their molt and a great many females sitting on their eggs, but as I had already made two long visits to this rookery and completed my records and taken a number of films, we did not waste any time on it.

We went on following the coastline, which was now becoming more difficult, for we could no longer drive full tilt across the fine sandy beach which stretched behind us all the way to Charlotte Point. The shore was now broken by bars of coarse shingle, which made hard going for our weasel. We had to go carefully to avoid ripping off the caterpillar tracks, which would have wasted a lot of time, winding about to find the best route, and crossing little streams which ran from the brackish tarns along the coast. That night we camped near Lake Marville.

It is the largest lake in the Kerguelen Islands, and is only a little above the level of the sea, from which it is divided by a narrow neck of land, cut by the stream overflowing from the lake. The ground here was so uneven that we were hardly able to find a large enough flat space to pitch our tents, for all this part of the coast is broken up by enormous tussocks of a large grass, known as *poa cooki*, which is common in most subantarctic islands. These tussocks are caused by erosion of the barer patches between clumps of grass, leaving large round mounds, divided by an irregular network of muddy ditches, which are constantly hollowed out by the rain and by the paths of inumerable crawling sea elephants.

We stuck to the coast until we reached Cape Digby, driving our weasel over sandy beaches, bars of shingle and fields of acaena grass. The cape is not very conspicuous; it is merely a cliff at the corner between the north and east coasts of the Courbet Peninsula. It is about fifty feet high, with steep terraces of rocky ledges inhabited by a large colony of cormorants, and is flanked on either side by two large rookeries of king penguins several hundred yards away.

The north coast, which we had now reached, consists

of a sheer rocky cliff about one hundred and fifty feet high, at the edge of a great undulating plain covered with acaena grass over which our weasel drove quite comfortably. Sometimes we had to make detours to avoid sharp rifts in the ground, and sometimes we had to cross screes of shingle, which were not good for our tracks, but on the whole we kept fairly close to the edge of the cliff and occasionally had a splendid view sheer down to the breaking sea.

We came round the shoulder of a large round hill and soon saw Mount Campbell, but we had an awkward drive winding across very uneven ground sliced up with ravines before we reached the foot of this fine rocky peak which dominates the country for miles around. Its northern face is a sheer cliff of bare rock on which Angot of an earlier mission did a beautiful climb in 1952. We found the remains of his camp at the bottom of the cliff.

From Mount Campbell we followed a deep and gently sloping ravine, until we came out on the coast near Cape Cotter. By this time I had had enough of being thrown about in the bumpy weasel, so I went on ahead of my companions, who had stopped to shoot rabbits on the slopes of the mountain. I walked along down a very pretty valley with a little stream running along its bed, and shortly before I reached the coast I was lucky enough to come upon a group of wandering albatrosses quietly going through the paces of their nuptial ceremony in the evening sunlight on a green lawn of acaena grass.

Many birds begin the mating season with a series of strange dances, during which they choose their mates. I spent a long time watching and filming a group of three of these splendid birds, who were so engrossed in their dance that they took not the slightest notice of me and let me approach to within two or three yards. There was one female, and two males who were presumably trying to outshine each other in beauty and elegance. They looked magnificent in their immaculate white plumage. Although these bulky creatures are so clumsy on the ground, their crude and unsophisticated dance is not without beauty. They turn slowly round, barely raising their feet from the ground, with their wings held out level, half spread, moving round in a circle and at the same time giving deep nods with their heads and snapping their beaks. Every now and then they stop dancing and one of the males moves a short distance away, leaving the couple sitting on the ground face to face. And they go on making the same strange nodding movements, snapping their beaks and uttering a sort of clucking sound, occasionally giving a touching and chaste kiss of beak against beak. Then the male who seemed to have been left out in the cold returns, the couple stand up and the dance goes on. The whole ceremony is perfectly good-mannered and without the least bickering or vulgar ill feeling. It has that aristocratic grace and distinction which is part of the albatross's character.

The arrival of our noisy little weasel and the approach of night put an end to this moving ceremony, and we hurriedly pitched our tents near the shore on a delightful lawn of grass through which a little stream ran.

As soon as I was up on the following morning I hurried over to the rookery of penguins from whose piercing cries and insidious stench we had suffered during the night, in spite of the shelter of the tent. It was for their sake that I had made this long trip, and I was anxious to study these birds at leisure. This part of the north coast of the Courbet Peninsula between Cape Cotter and Betsy Cove is the only place on the island where macaroni penguins (*Eudyptes chrysolophus*) have so far been found. This species and the emperor penguin are the most southerly of their family. In the antarctic it also breeds in South Shetland, South Georgia, the South Orkneys, Prince Edward Island, Marion Island, Heard Island — all to the south of Kerguelen.

This colony of macaroni penguins, which covers

about a dozen miles of favored coastline, is probably the largest concentration of penguins anywhere in the world. It was previously visited by Angot in February 1952 and by Aubert de la Rüe in November of the same year. They reported five rookeries between Cape Cotter and Accessible Bay, and de la Rüe estimated their numbers as: one hundred thousand, two hundred and fifty thousand, two hundred thousand, four hundred thousand and forty thousand, making a total of almost a million. Of course these figures are not exact, but they do give an idea of the density of the penguin population within a small area. I had no difficulty in recognizing the different colonies recorded by my predecessors; and we made a rough census of their numbers, which agreed fairly closely with de la Rüe's.

The macaroni penguin, like the more common rock hopper, has a black-and-yellow crest; but instead of sticking out on either side, it lies on top of the head and runs straight backwards.

Aubert de la Rüe noted that these birds lay their eggs in November. Incubation cannot take very long, for when I visited these rookeries in January the chicks were all hatched and were already about half the size of their parents. They were covered with down, black on the back and wings and white on the breast and belly; their crests had not yet appeared. As usual, they were all gathered together in the middle of the rookery, where the adults could keep an eye on them.

There were also a good many colonies of cormorants on the north coast of the Courbet Peninsula, often completely surrounded by the milling rookeries of macaroni penguins, and usually on outcrops of rock among the penguins' more level colonies. I had often watched cormorants in the many little colonies around Port-aux-Français, but this was the first time I had seen them bringing up their young. They were fascinating to watch, but to do so I had to flounder through a stinking bog of mud and guano.

When we visited them the cormorant colonies contained about a hundred and fifty to two hundred adult birds. The eggs had all been hatched and there were large numbers of chicks. The nests are carefully made of seaweed and built up some height from the ground; they are used for several broods, and every year the parents add a little more seaweed and build them a little higher.

It is most interesting to see the young being fed. The chicks can neither fly nor fish, so the parents have to go fishing for them. Then they come back, regurgitate the food in their stomachs, and feed their young with a pap consisting chiefly of small molluscs. It took me several hours to make a satisfactory film of the young ones being stuffed with their parents' vomit. It was a great strain on my patience and my nerves. There was no lack of young birds being fed, but they were scattered about all over the rookery. The moment I saw a parent beginning to retch I would make for the spot, staggering and slipping on the guano and the seaweed, in order to film a close-up of the scene. But nine times out of ten I got there just as the meal was over, for it takes only a few seconds. And then I saw that I could have taken a splendid close-up from the place I had just left. It was quite maddening. At last, after stumbling all over the colony in pursuit of feeding birds, I managed to take a few good sequences; but not until I had covered myself with mud and guano and picked up a vile smell from which I and my unfortunate companions suffered for the rest of the trip.

The young cormorants are always hungry, and as soon as their parents return from fishing they start nagging at them with their bills, which they try to insert into their parents' mouths. The old birds do not usually give in at once, presumably in order to give their catch time to digest, but at last the young ones get their way. Then the old bird opens its beak very wide, and the chick's head vanishes into its parent's gullet. The old bird now begins to make vomiting movements so that the chick can suck up its half-digested nourishment almost from its parent's stomach. It was a touching scene, and I could not help pitying the parent birds, which are constantly having to suffer this uncomfortable business, for their young are never satisfied and are forever clamoring for another meal.

I spent a whole day watching the colonies of penguins and cormorants, and came away with a large number of valuable films, photographs and notes. That night we camped not far from Betsy Cove, the first indentation in Accessible Bay.

Our journey back to Port-aux-Français next day was quite an adventure. It was the first time that this piece of country had been crossed in a weasel, and we had been strongly advised against it by those who had tried it before. The whole country is a wilderness of stone; there are huge boulders, ravines, streams, steep ridges of rock, with occasional lakes and bogs — in fact it would be hard to find worse country for a weasel. We suffered as much as our weasel did, for we had to reconnoiter the ground carefully before trying to drive across it, which meant that we covered the whole route twice over, to say nothing of countless false starts and detours. After reconnoitering a piece of ground we drove the weasel slowly forward, guided by two scouts on foot, who had to move the larger boulders with a crowbar.

The route was very hard to follow, and it was easy to

Prelude to a New Adventure

get lost in the middle of a maze of little valleys and
ridges of rock. At last we came to the top of a small
rounded hill from which we could see the southern
coast of the Courbet Peninsula, which we reached after
a few more hours of strenuous work. This was familiar
country, a little to the west of Port-aux-Français. We
were all dead beat after this four-day expedition, but
we had the satisfaction of bringing back a large haul of
valuable films, photographs and notes, both on the biology and the geology of a little-known part of Kerguelen. We had also found a route which would be very
useful to future expeditions to the north coast, and
meant that one could now reach Betsy Cove from Port-
aux-Français in one day, whereas the old coastal route
took two.

When we got back to the station we were welcomed
by the good news that the *Kista Dan* was approaching
Heard Island and would reach us in a few days. My
stay in Kerguelen was really over.

CHAPTER SIX

Retrospect and Prospect

B EFORE leaving Kerguelen I must say a few words about the mission's program and how far it has been accomplished. Its purpose, as we have already seen, was to reaffirm French sovereignty, establish a base and meteorological station, see whether it was possible to build an airfield or resuscitate the sealing industry and to carry out biological and geological research.

French sovereignty is firmly established and the base long since built, but the airfield has not proceeded at all far. The Courbet Peninsula has been surveyed for a site and a hangar has been brought to Port-aux-Français, but it has never been put up because of the strength of the wind. There is still much controversy about the value of an airfield on Kerguelen. It would, of course, be a useful stopping place, since it lies on the direct line between Cape Town and Perth, but it is a difficult place for flying and landing because of the continual violent gales. Moreover, the regular air service, which has been operating since 1952, has preferred to take a longer but far more clement route by way of the Cocos Islands, a long way to the north. If there were a third world war a strategic air base on Kerguelen might be very useful, but I hope that there is no need of one at the moment, and in any case if it were to be fully manned and equipped it would be too costly for France to provide without aid.

There was an idea of extracting certain chemicals from the vast quantity of laminarian seaweed around the coasts, but analysis showed that they were not present in large enough percentages to be useful, especially as they would have to be carried so far to find a market. Aubert de la Rüe found that the subsoil was practically barren, and there are very few fish in the sea round Kerguelen — we hardly ever had fresh fish to eat — unlike New Amsterdam, where fish and crayfish abound.

The one trade on the island which might prove lucrative is sea-elephant hunting — but it would have to be strictly controlled, and not repeat the indiscriminate slaughter of the past. Control would not reduce the output in the long run. In the Falkland Islands the production of oil has been maintained in spite of strict limitations on the number of animals killed. Indeed, with improved methods of extracting the oil, production has even been increased. It would not be easy to enforce controls in Kerguelen — for the difficult country and vile weather tend to make parts of the island inaccessible — and a good deal of research would have to be done before we knew exactly what the controls should be. Moreover, the market price of oil is none too stable.

Kerguelen is therefore unlikely ever to be profitable industrially, but it may still be important to science. Many important physical problems concerning the weather, the variation in gravitational force and the nature of the ionosphere may be solved from evidence obtained in the Southern Hemisphere. A remarkably large number of expeditions are to be sent to the antarctic during the International Geophysical Year of 1957, and they may well find the base at Kerguelen extremely useful.

It is time to reconsider the work of the French mission. So far it has been chiefly engaged in building the base and in geophysical research. Geology and biology have been comparatively neglected; they have no laboratories as yet on the station, and the means of traveling about the islands are still inadequate. There is no seagoing boat attached to the mission for oceanographic work and coastal voyages.

Now that the building is nearly over, most of the soldiers and engineers on the island could well be sent home. A smaller garrison, chiefly of scientists, with only

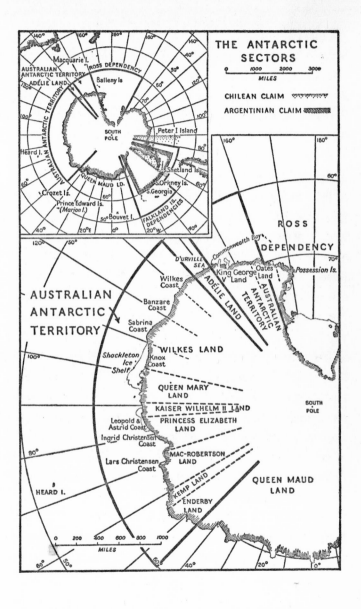

THE ANTARCTIC
SECTORS

0   1000   2000   3000
MILES

CHILEAN CLAIM
ARGENTINIAN CLAIM

a few technicians to keep the base going, would make for a happier atmosphere.

So much for Kerguelen. My new expedition was to Mac-Robertson and Princess Elizabeth Lands in the Australian Sectors, and I must explain what these sectors are and how these lands were discovered.

It is only comparatively recently that the countries which have explored the antarctic have been interested in annexing land on that vast, white and apparently useless continent. About fifty years ago they began to compete in the whaling industry and to need land bases, and since then the competition has become keener. Great Britain took the first step by creating the Falkland Islands Dependencies in 1908, followed by the Ross Dependencies in 1917.

But most of the whaling companies are Norwegian, and in other companies many of the men are Norwegians. To avoid having to pay British taxes, Norway annexed in 1929 the Bouvet and Peter I Islands and a part of Enderby Land, where she set up her own bases.

But what is the international law about these annexations? The general principle is that mere discovery of virgin territory is not enough. It must be effectively occupied — as for instance with Kerguelen. But it is not easy to occupy polar territory, and other means of appropriation have to be found.

Retrospect and Prospect

Discovery is often thought to give a right to antarctic territory provided that an official act is issued and duly ratified. But this principle is difficult to apply because discoveries often overlap and it is hard to say where a territory begins and ends. It has therefore generally been superseded by the system of sectors, which was originally created to deal with the arctic, where the area within the Arctic Circle is divided into sectors and apportioned to the country through which the corresponding section of the Arctic Circle passes. This cannot be done in the antarctic, for none of the interested countries is anywhere near the Antarctic Circle. The sectors are therefore claimed by right of discovery, each country annexing the triangle between the South Pole and the stretch of antarctic coast discovered by its citizens. The system is imperfect because land is often discovered independently by more than one country; besides, it takes no account of the principle of occupation.

If the country cannot be occupied, some form of control strengthens the claim to ownership. In polar regions the usual requirements of international law have been much relaxed. The agents of the sovereign state no longer need to reside in the territory. They may govern from a distance and only exercise their authority on occasional visits and expeditions. But of course effective occupation is far better, for it makes ownership incontestable. When bases are established on the Antarctic Continent it is to carry out scientific research and explore the hinterland, but their chiefs are also invested with administrative powers, so that they can also be said to exercise official control as their countries' representatives.

But these sectors have more political than legal importance. Some countries recognize them as established by law which should be universally recognized, while others consider it a temporary arrangement, with no legal sanction and kept up by courtesy rather than law.

The first sector was annexed by Great Britain. There are now six. Five of them belong to Great Britain, Norway, Australia, New Zealand and France. The French Sector is only a tiny piece of Adélie Land which is sandwiched in the Australian Sector. The sixth sector has not yet been claimed. The map shows the limits of the sectors and the dates they were annexed.

But these sectors have never been internationally recognized. The United States has protested on four separate occasions against annexations of sectors in the antarctic and the principle of ownership by right of discovery. They will recognize only permanent and effective occupation. In 1948 the United States State Department opened negotiations with the seven countries which had claimed antarctic territory (Argentina, Australia, Chile, France, New Zealand, Norway and the United Kingdom) and recommended that all antarctic territories should be internationalized to facilitate scientific research. Argentina and Chile have made more violent protests, claiming that geographically the Falkland Islands Dependencies in the British Sector really belong to them. The protests were bitter, and it seemed possible at one time that they might lead to war, for the Chilean and Argentinian claims not only infringed British territory, but also overlapped one another.

The system of sectors seems to be on the way out. More and more permanent bases are being set up in the antarctic every year, and they will probably settle who owns that continent.

I must now give a brief history of the Australian Sector of the Antarctic, especially Mac-Robertson and Princess Elizabeth Lands, to which our expedition was going.

Enderby Land was the first to be discovered — by John Biscoe, a master whaler of the English company Enderby Brothers, on February 28, 1831. He was circumnavigating the Antarctic Continent on the *Tula* when he sighted a rocky point, which he named Cape Ann, and shortly afterwards a coastline stretching northeast. He could not get within less than twenty-five miles of this land, which he named Enderby Land, after his owners. Two years later the coast to the east of Enderby Land was discovered by Peter Kemp, captain of the brig *Magnet* of the same company. This is now Kemp Land.

In 1838 – 1839 John Balleny, leader of the British expedition on the *Sabrina*, visited the other end of what is now the Australian Sector. Here he discovered the islands which now bear his name and a strip of coast to which he gave the name of his ship.

The French Adélie Land is sandwiched within the Australian Sector. It was discovered on January 20, 1840, by Dumont d'Urville during the expedition of the *Astrolabe* and *Zélée*. He did not go ashore, and it was not until 1912 that Mawson landed in Adélie Land and set up a base on Cape Denison in nearby King George V Land.

A week after Dumont d'Urville's visit, Charles Wilkes, commanding the United States Exploring Expedition, confirmed the discovery. He was only forty-two days in the Antarctic, but during that time he discovered two other "lands." One of them is now called by his name and is the largest territory in the Australian Sector. The other, which he christened Knox Land, is now known as Knox Coast and included in Wilkes Land.

Then there was a long interval until 1901, when the German explorer E. von Drygalski, whose ship, the

Gauss, was forced to winter in the ice, discovered Kaiser Wilhelm II Land. Finally in 1912, while Captain Scott was on his tragic dash to the South Pole, one of his base parties, working from Cape Adare, discovered Oates Land, the most westerly part of the present Australian Sector.

We now come to the modern phase of antarctic exploration. In December 1929 the *Norvegia* was driven by the pack ice to within ninety miles of Enderby Land, and Captain Riiser-Larsen, the most celebrated polar pilot of the time, made a reconnaissance flight during which he succeeded in landing on the coast of Enderby Land. A further flight in January 1930 enabled him to draw the first map of the western coast of this territory.

In 1926 the British Commonwealth Conference had proposed to annex, by right of discovery, all the antarctic territory between Enderby Land in the west and Oates Land in the east, except for Adélie Land, which was recognized as a French possession. The region therefore had to be properly surveyed, and so in 1929 Sir Douglas Mawson, who had already made two successful expeditions to the antarctic, was put in charge of a new expedition known as the BANZARE (British, Australian, New Zealand Antarctic Research Expedition). Scott's old ship, the *Discovery*, was put at his disposal.

But this was the time of the slump, funds were short

and the expedition would have been abandoned had not a rich Australian businessman, MacPherson Robertson, better known as Mac-Robertson, offered the committee ten thousand pounds. Mawson selected his staff from members of his previous expeditions, together with an able team of scientists, and the *Discovery* sailed from London to meet the expedition at Cape Town.

After touching at the islands of Crozet, Possession, Kerguelen and Heard, the *Discovery* entered the pack ice on December 7. On December 29, 1929, and January 4, 1930, two reconnaissances were made by air, and a rugged land was discovered, entirely covered with ice, with several ranges of mountains near the coast. Offshore there were several small islands partly free of snow. This new land was named Mac-Robertson Land in honor of the expedition's benefactor.

On January 13 the *Discovery* anchored before the great promontory which forms the northern point of Enderby Land, and which was named Cape Batterbee. Mawson, accompanied by a party of scientists, landed on a rocky island near the coast. They hoisted the Union Jack and built a cairn, in which they placed a sealed document officially annexing Enderby, Kemp and Mac-Robertson Lands in the name of the Australian Government. This little island was appropriately named Proclamation Island. They sailed round Cape Batterbee,

Cape Close and Cape Ann, and on January 14 they were surprised to find, on the very edge of the area they were exploring, the *Norvegia* with Lars Christensen's Norwegian Antarctic Expedition. The two expeditions exchanged signals, and Riiser-Larsen came on board the *Discovery* and there was a friendly conference between the two leaders, who agreed upon the frontier between the Australian and Norwegian Sectors. This decision was of great value to future research in the area. The *Discovery* completed her survey of the coast between longitude 45° and 75° east, and arrived back in Australia on March 21, 1930.

On November 22 of the same year another expedition left Hobart in the same ship and still under the leadership of Sir Douglas Mawson. After calling at MacQuarie Island and suffering various delays, the *Discovery* ran into a terrible storm lasting for six days, during which she was several times in grave danger, but eventually on January 4, 1931, the expedition reached Cape Denison on the coast of King George V Land, where Mawson had passed two successive winters twenty years before. The Union Jack was again hoisted and the territory formally annexed in the name of the Australian Government. Leaving Cape Denison, the *Discovery* sailed westwards along the coast of Adélie Land. On January 7 Wilkes Land was sighted from the air, but the ship was held up by thick pack ice in the waters which Mawson had named d'Urville Sea. On January 15 and 16 two more air reconnaissances were made, new land was sighted, next to Wilkes Land, with a coastline extending southwest. This was named Banzare Land.

During the following days a series of storms severely damaged the airplane and prevented Mawson from making flights over Knox Land. But the airplane was repaired, and during a reconnaissance on February 9 new land was discovered at latitude 66° 30′ south, longitude 76° east, which Mawson baptized Princess Elizabeth Land. On February 11 they sighted the coastline, which was dominated by uneven uplands and sloped away to the south. The ship was able to approach this coast near a cape, which was named Cape Darnley, after the chairman of the *Discovery* committee. When they rounded this cape they were surprised to find a large bay of ice-free water stretching southwards as far as latitude 69° south. These waters were duly reconnoitered from the air and named after Captain MacKenzie, who commanded the *Discovery*. Mawson would have liked to explore them more thoroughly, but it was too late in the season and coal was running low. There was no pack ice beyond longitude 70° east, so they were able to hug the coast of Mac-Robertson Land and to plot the coastline. On February 13 a party landed on the Scullin Monolith, one of the rare rocky points on this coast, where the British flag was again hoisted and the territory formally annexed.

In spite of the bad weather, various features of Mac-Robertson Land were noted and named, including four ranges of mountains called after Masson, David, Casey and Henderson, members of the *Discovery* committee, and a great rocky peak which was named after Hugh Robert Mill, a celebrated writer on the antarctic. On February 18 another landing was made, this time on Cape Bruce, and scientific observations taken, after which the *Discovery* headed for Tasmania and reached Hobart on March 19, 1931.

This expedition had plotted twenty-five hundred miles of coastline between Mac-Robertson Land and King George V Land and provided the basis of the act of February 7, 1933, fixing the boundaries of the sector and annexing it in the name of the Commonwealth.

At about the same time as Mawson was making his voyages of discovery a flotilla of Norwegian whalers fitted out by Lars Christensen was operating in the same area and adding to the knowledge of the Australian and Norwegian Sectors. They reconnoitered the coast of Enderby, Kemp and Mac-Robertson Lands as well as Cape Darnley and the Scullin and Murray Monoliths, and they landed on the hitherto unexplored southern shore of the MacKenzie Sea, which they named Lars Christensen Land.

The Norwegians continued their exploration of the Australian Sector during the great cruises round the antarctic which Lars Christensen and Klarius Mikkelsen made on the *Thorshavn* in 1933 and 1935. During the summer of 1933 – 1934 they flew over the coast of Lars Christensen Land and into Mac-Robertson Land; and Princess Astrid Land (now King Leopold and Queen Astrid Coast) was discovered from the air.

In 1934 – 1935 Lars Christensen discovered in Princess Elizabeth Land what he named the Ingrid Christensen Coast, after his daughter, who, like her mother, was accompanying him on the voyage. He landed on the part of the coast now known as the Vestfold Hills. As a result of these explorations a map of the Australian and Norwegian Sectors was published which is by far the best that we possess today.

The following summer (1935 – 1936) the oceanic research vessel *William Scoresby*, belonging to Discovery Investigations, explored the coast of the MacKenzie Sea, Mac-Robertson and Kemp Lands west of longitude 57°. This expedition discovered the King Edward VIII Sound on the coast of Kemp and Rayner Land. It landed also at the Scullin Monolith and Bertha Island in William Scoresby Bay in Kemp Land.

Retrospect and Prospect

During the summer of 1936 – 1937 Lars Christensen's fleet again visited the Australian Sector. Christensen had the whole coast between Kaiser Wilhelm II Land and Proclamation Island surveyed from the air. He also landed on the Scullin Monolith, which few visitors seem able to resist. Here he established a triangulation point. Meanwhile another of his vessels, the *Thorshavn*, visited the King Leopold and Queen Astrid Coast, but without landing.

In 1938 – 1939 Lincoln Ellsworth, commanding the *Wyatt Earp* of the United States Antarctic Expedition, visited Princess Elizabeth Land and succeeded in landing on the coast of Vestfold Hills and on the Svenner and Rauer groups of islands near the coast. A reconnaissance flight penetrated as far as latitude 72° south longitude 79° east, and this region was annexed by the United States and named American Highland.

Finally during the summer of 1946 – 1947, in the course of Operation "High Jump" of the United States Navy Antarctic Expedition under the command of Admiral Byrd, by far the largest enterprise ever undertaken in the antarctic, a number of reconnaissances were made in the Australian Sector, though no wintering parties were left on the continent. The western group of the expedition made a very thorough aerial survey of the coasts of the Australian and neighboring sectors between longitude 170° and 10° east, and the photographs they took enabled Dr. Law and the captain of our ship to pick a site which looked suitable for the Australian base. It is now high time that we set out on this expedition.

CHAPTER SEVEN

Southward Bound

O N January 22, I thought the day would never end.
We knew that the *Kista Dan* had left Heard Island
the day before; she should take twenty hours to cover
the three-hundred-mile run to Kerguelen, so we expected
her to arrive at any moment. I spent the afternoon, like
Sister Anne, scanning the Passe Royale, but there was
no sign of a ship, and eventually the dinner bell put an
end to my barren vigil. But when I came out of the mess
I saw a small spot of white on the dark background of
Morbihan Bay. It moved, it grew. There was no longer
any doubt. It was the ship we were waiting for.

The camp was bubbling over with excitement. Armengaud, the chief of the Kerguelen mission, Redonnet, the
quartermaster, Georges Schwartz and I went on board
the *Gros-Ventre*, and reached the *Kista Dan* just as she
was mooring in the bay not far from Port-aux-Français.
Dr. Philip Law, Director of the Australian National Antarctic Research Expedition, met us as we came on board,

[145]

and introduced us to his chief colleagues: Bob Dovers, leader of the wintering party; Macey, his second; Dr. Gwynn, the ornithologist; Dick Thomson, the quartermaster; as well as Captain Petersen of the *Kista Dan*, and the chief engineer. We were cordially received by the Australians in the saloon. They were a very congenial set of people, friendly and straightforward, and the ship was clean and comfortable. There was plenty of excellent whisky, so it was late before we went ashore, brimming over with optimism, and stumbled over the maze of oil drums and packing cases on the landing stage on our way back to our gloomy quarters in Port-aux-Français.

Loading began next morning. Most of the gear had been put on board at Melbourne; we had merely to complete it with six hundred drums of petrol and fuel oil, an amphibian weasel and a hundred cases of rations and equipment, which had been brought by the *Saint-Marcouf*. Finally there were sixty tons of fresh water for use on the voyage. Dr. Law was in a great hurry to get away, as the summer was already far advanced and we had not a day to lose if we were to get safely through the pack ice. Everyone worked furiously, but after thirty-six hours we had to stop because of a violent storm. All the time we were loading we did not have a single whole day of fine weather; short spells of calm were followed by squalls, which made it difficult, if not impossible, to work afloat.

In spite of this filthy weather, we did not take long to get all the fuel and other cargo loaded, but we had much more trouble with the fresh water. The *Kista Dan* could not come within reach of the landing stage, for the water was too shallow and the sea too rough, so all the fresh water had to be brought down to the quayside in tankers, where the fire pump transferred it into the landing craft, which had been filled with water tanks. With this unruly load, the landing craft was very heavy, unstable and hard to handle. In rough weather she rolled dangerously, with her top-heavy load of fresh water slopping about, and became a savage and ungovernable monster trying to smash anything within her reach. When at last she was safely tethered alongside the ship, her load had to be pumped out into the ship's water tanks, and this slow task could be done only in a flat calm. Various other methods were tried without success, and once the captain took the ship to Port Jeanne-d'Arc to see if he could make use of the old system used for watering whalers, but found that it was ruined and could not be made to work.

This problem was made even more serious because each day of bad weather increased the amount of water needed and added to the delay. The ship used about three tons of water a day for cooking, washing and supplying the men and dogs. So every day's delay meant that our required load of sixty tons had to be increased by another three. It was like the Danaïdes carrying water in sieves. The bad weather, which was the despair of the staff, gave the men a chance to rest after their hard work. We had all sorts of parties and celebrations, which gave the members of the two missions, as well as the crew of the *Kista Dan,* opportunities to meet and get to know one another around well-laden tables and beside a hospitable bar in a warm and friendly saloon echoing to a chorus of French, Australian and Danish songs bellowed in an extraordinary mixture of different accents, and with all the usual sailor's gusto, to Dr. Law's skillful accompaniment on the accordion.

There were twenty-two men on the Australian expedition. I have already mentioned Dr. Law and Bob Dovers. The first is the director of the antarctic department in the Australian Ministry of External Affairs, as well as head of the ANARE. As physicist in charge of cosmic-ray research, he was on the *Wyatt Earp* Expedition which in 1947 failed to reach Commonwealth Bay in King George V Land because of the unusual amount of pack ice. In 1950 he spent some time in Queen Maud Land as Australian observer attached to the Anglo-Norwegian *Norsel* Expedition, and paid several visits to Heard and

Macquarie Islands. His thorough and untiring organization of this new expedition was largely responsible for its success.

Dovers is a familiar name in the history of antarctic exploration. Bob's father, George Dovers, was on Mawson's famous and ill-fated expedition to Adélie Land in 1911 and spent the winter at the second base. He was also one of the eight men on Frank Wild's expedition, which, although it had no dogs or motor vehicles, managed to survey and map five hundred miles of the antarctic coast in five months. Bob Dovers is a geophysicist like his father. Although he was only thirty-one, he was a veteran of the antarctic. In 1947 – 1948 he wintered at Heard Island with the first Australian mission and there did much valuable survey work. He spent four months of the summer of 1948 – 1949 on Macquarie Island, and he stayed in Adélie Land from December 1951 to January 1953 as an observer with the French. This gave him much useful experience in working with huskies and sledges. He is the perfect type of polar explorer — courageous, efficient and extremely tough.

The twenty-seven sled dogs on the *Kista Dan* had a story worth telling. When the first French expedition to Adélie Land, which sailed in the *Commandant Charcot*, returned to Australia after failing to get through the pack ice, they found that the Australian regulations forbade them to land the dogs. The press made a lot of fuss about it, but the authorities relaxed their ban only enough to allow the dogs to be temporarily lodged in the Melbourne Zoo until they were taken off to Adélie Land by the second expedition in 1950. The puppies born in Australia were left behind together with a few adults as a present in recognition of their kind treatment in Melbourne. After a while all these dogs, young and old, were taken to Heard Island to get them accustomed to the cold, and it was their descendants that we were now taking to Mac-Robertson Land. They belonged to the two great races of polar dogs, Labradors and Greenlanders, and among them were crossbreeds from the two stocks. For the time being they were shut up in their kennels on the deck, with nothing to amuse them except occasional visits from men on Kerguelen and a short walk on deck at mealtimes.

I often used to go and look at them, for they were splendid beasts, tough, strongly built and very intelligent. At first I was a little nervous of going too near them, probably because of the savage reputation they have been given by some polar explorers. But they do not deserve this reputation, except when they have been starved and beaten by natives and trappers in the north.

This treatment is enough to make any dog savage, es-

The celebrated Kerguelen cabbage, much valued by the old navigators as a tonic against scurvy.

They gravely looked me up and down with dignified curiosity.

The little base of Port-aux-Français at Kerguelen in summer, with its barraく huts and stony ground.

The base in winter.

A young sea elephant.

…t when they are not fully grown, albatrosses have an enormous wingspread. …uelen is one of the few places where one can lift a sitting bird off her nest, …ine her eggs, and put her back without alarming her in the least.

The giant, or "stinking," petrel is a little smaller than the albatross. Its shifty greenish-gray eyes and its long thin feet make it an ugly and repellent sight on

Dogsleds, with weasels and barges in the background.

wo rockhoppers investigating a movie camera. They are the smallest of
e penguins on Kerguelen.

Kerguelen is a country of extremes.

The *Kista Dan* in the ice
her way to Mac-Robertson
Land.

It needed two days of hard
work before we got her free
. . . by the absurdly primitive
method of smashing the ice
by hand with boat hooks and
spikes and shoving it back
out of the way.

A dreamlike landscape.

The author on the coast of the antarctic continent near the Australian base at Mawson.

A crumbling cathedral of ice.

Beautifully shaped pancake ice, which oscillated gently with the swell
made the sea look as if it were covered with gigantic white water lilie

pecially since the climate and the work they do give them enormous appetites. But if they are well looked after, well-fed, treated like friends and punished only when they deserve it, they are the most intelligent, engaging and affectionate creatures.

It is true that they sometimes quarrel pretty savagely with one another, but it is all part of their work of drawing a sled. Every team has its leader, who is perfectly conscious of his own dignity and importance, and it is part of his job to keep rivals in their place. A sharp and well-placed bite is the best way of showing who is master and bullying an idle or undisciplined teammate into obedience. It is important to know these rivalries when making up teams of dogs, for some will never get on together, and others will work only under a particular leader. But once this has been taken into account, the dogs will work hard. A team of nine can go on pulling a sled weighing some seven hundred pounds for more than thirty miles over rough ground for day after day, and in emergencies they will do double the distance.

When visiting the dogs I also explored the rest of the ship, and as she is an important figure in the expedition I must describe her in some detail. The S.S. *Kista Dan*, chartered by the Australian Government from J. Lauritzen of Copenhagen, was built in 1952 at Aalborg. She is two hundred and fourteen feet long and thirty-six feet in beam; she draws sixteen feet of water and her displacement is twelve hundred tons. Her Diesel motors develop fifteen hundred horsepower and she can do twelve knots at speed.

She is a mixed passenger and cargo boat with accommodation for twenty-four passengers. She was specially built for sailing through ice and has several special features. Her reinforced hull is rounded and her stem raised slightly above water level, so that it slides up over the ice and smashes through it under the ship's weight. On each side of the screw and astern of the rudder there are metal fins to protect them and also to cut the ice.

The crow's nest is very comfortable, and electrically heated. It contains duplicates of all the controls on the bridge, so that the captain can take complete charge of the ship from this high lookout post. The holds are very large and can be loaded quickly with one fifteen-ton derrick and four five-tonners. The saloon is extremely comfortable and the cabins roomy. They have large bay windows and electric heating — a very great comfort in polar weather.

Captain Petersen is one of the greatest experts in polar navigation. He has for long been in command of whalers and has made several expeditions to Greenland and the antarctic.

We were carrying a large cargo: five prefabricated

huts for the winter base; a year's food and supplies, including a lot of scientific equipment; an electric power-plant; three weasels; and, finally, two reconnaissance aircraft, one of which was lashed down onto a cradle on the quarter-deck and the other dismantled in the hold. They were Auster VI airplanes with one hundred and fifty horsepower motors and could cruise at from seventy to eighty miles per hour, with a ceiling of nine thousand feet. They could be fitted with wheels, floats or skis, and their airborne duration was about three hours with floats and almost four hours with wheels or skis.

Dr. Law told me more about the expedition. It had to find a suitable site for the winter base in the Australian Sector between longitude 55° and 85° east. They would need an exposed area of rock on which to build their huts. It had to be near the sea or the barrier ice, conveniently placed for studying the weather and the biology of the area, and also accessible to the great plateau inland so that they could go off on expeditions by weasel or by sled. The site which Schwartz had told me of seemed most suitable and was eventually chosen. It lay on longitude 63° east.

The watering team had to build a permanent camp, make a biological survey and also a magnetic survey, as well as observe the weather and do other scientific research. Schwartz was oceanographer to the party be-

[153]

sides having to look after the dogs and organize sled parties. For in the spring they intended to go off on excursions for as much as three hundred miles in order to collect geographical information, so there was plenty to do.

On Wednesday, January 27, 1954, loading the *Kista Dan* was at last complete. At six in the evening Georges and I went on board for the last time, with all our friends who had come to see me off, and two hours later the ship weighed anchor. We were really off! The moment I had been longing for had come at last. I went onto the upper deck and watched the ship make her ritual circuit of Chaner Island before heading out for the Passe Royale. I was moved to see the lights of Port-aux-Français fading in the night. My year in this little station had passed all too quickly, and I had enjoyed it in spite of certain difficulties, inevitable when men are forcibly cooped up together. Our speed increased and the lights of the station disappeared behind Guite Point. The night was cold and damp, and the dinner bell summoned me down to the saloon.

As soon as we were through the Passe Royale and out of the shelter of Morbihan Bay we headed south and began to feel the great ocean swell. The first four days of the voyage were most unpleasant. The weather was frankly vile, the sky gray and lowering, and one could see nothing. A westerly gale was blowing and the ship rolled heavily in the high seas. The curved lines of her hull were beautifully designed for smashing a way through ice, but they made her pitch and roll vilely in open water.

The temperature fell hour by hour. When we left Kerguelen it was 50° F., but before long the thermometer was down at freezing point, showing that we had crossed the antarctic convergence into the antarctic zone. I have already mentioned how we crossed the subtropical convergence on the way from Tamatave to Kerguelen. The change of temperature is just as sudden in both cases and the cause is the same. The appearance of the water also changes as one leaves the warmer blue seas, which are poor in plankton, and enters the cold green waters where the plankton is very dense and rich in diatoms. This is why whales, which live chiefly on plankton, are so numerous in the antarctic.

As we sailed southwards we met a new range of birds. At first we saw the usual Kerguelen birds — skuas, giant petrels, sooty and wandering albatrosses — but further south they gradually gave place to antarctic petrels, Cape pigeons and other polar birds.

In spite of bad weather and rough seas the *Kista Dan* maintained her course and her normal speed of twelve knots. On the evening of the 28th, twenty-four hours after leaving Kerguelen, we were level with Heard Island, but too far away to see it. On the 31st, in latitude 64° south, we caught sight of our first icebergs — a few growlers (or small irregular bergs) to start with and then several great flat-topped bergs. More of them appeared later in the day, and their massive outlines stood out against the sky. It was a beautiful evening and the sky above the southern horizon shone with the white glow of the "ice blink" — the reflection of a distant ice field. One sees the glow long before the ice itself is visible. To starboard we saw the lights of two Norwegian whalers.

I was deeply moved by the beauty of the scene and these first signs that we were now in the antarctic, but my joy was mixed with a slight disappointment, for we had already reached latitude 65° 30′ south, and if we kept up the same speed we should be in sight of Mac-Robertson Land the next day and ready to land. It would of course be excellent for the captain and the landing party to save so much precious time, and I was glad for their sakes, but I did not want to reach our destination so soon. I had been looking forward so much to the prospect of steaming through the pack ice, to the splendid scenery, to the difficulty and excitement of it all, and to the adventure of a polar expedition that I had dreamed of so long, that I felt that I should be cheated if we arrived too quickly and met no obstacles on the way. I believe that in spite of their haste to reach their goal and begin work, the Australians, and even Dr. Law himself, shared something of this feeling.

CHAPTER EIGHT

Through the Ice

BY midnight the ship was going dead slow. Numbers of growlers floated round us; I gathered that the pack was only a few miles ahead and that we should soon be coming into it. My fears had been groundless, and it looked as if my wishes would be fulfilled, perhaps more than fulfilled. I was so excited by this news that I could not get to sleep and spent the rest of the night staring through the big window in my cabin at the chunks of ice, large and small, that floated past our hull in the clear pure night. Whenever we hit one of the larger lumps, the ship shook from stem to stern.

At five o'clock I went up on deck and watched the sun rise with a dazzling brilliance; it was a little like a dawn in the tropics, although we had left them so far behind. We had now entered the pack ice, and the scene was unforgettably lovely. The ship steamed slowly through an ocean of ice which reached as far as the eye could see. It was an indescribable chaos of ice blocks of every size, their white surfaces glistening or dull as they lay in sun or shadow, with here and there sheets of open water, a string of dark-blue patches, so dark they seemed almost black.

We had around us every type of polar ice: slender pieces, carved by the melting heat of the sun, which floated elegantly by like great swans of supernatural whiteness; treacherous growlers almost entirely immersed; reefs of hard greenish ice; floes — or broken sheets of ice — sliding and colliding, and sometimes piling up in thick layers; and icebergs of every possible shape.

These icebergs are enormous hunks which have broken away from the great glaciers that cover the Antarctic Continent. For a long time they preserve their original shape — huge cubes of ice standing more than one hundred feet out of the water . They are often more than one hundred yards long, and their submerged volume is about six times as much as that which appears above the suface. They have a regular rectangular shape with straight sides and a flat level top. In shadow they look chalky white, but the sunlight makes them reflect the most delicate colors.

They break off from the parent glacier in the spring thaw and then drift for months, often being carried far up into the warm waters of the tropics. But they do not all remain square. Many of them capsize when their foundations melt or are worn away, and then one sees their bases, chiseled and carved by the sea into the most extraordinary shapes — pinnacles, glistening cathedrals of crystal, or crumbling fortresses with jagged bastions — and pitted with deep mysterious caverns.

The beauty of this dreamlike architecture is enhanced by the sun, which floods its whiteness with dazzling rays, tints it with all the colors of the rainbow, lights the caverns of ice, dyes the broken edges of floes a deep blue or a pale green, and makes hidden spurs shimmer sea-green beneath the water.

The weather was perfect, without a breath of wind, and the temperature very mild — hardly below freezing point. The sea, subdued by the mass of ice that covered it, had become perfectly calm — a pleasant change after the heavy swell of the last few days. Everyone came up on deck to enjoy the lovely weather and the extraordinary landscape — a novel sight for most of us. Cameras came out of hiding and hardly stopped clicking for the rest of the voyage. The world of ice was a revelation to me. No amount of books and photographs and films can begin to give one a real idea of the incredible splendor and the wonderful beauty of this polar landscape. It is a world apart: a mineral world, frozen and yet alive, a terrifying universe, quite outside human range, where one feels a stranger, lost and defenseless but for the comfort of the ship to which one clings with both hands.

But this wilderness of ice is not utterly deserted. I saw a few Adélie penguins, ludicrous little figures hopping from floe to floe, and two emperor penguins, with their slow and solemn gait, who gazed curiously but unafraid at the strange ship as it passed them by. I also saw some Weddell and crab-eating seals sprawling on a large floe and raising their broad mustached faces in astonishment, but making no effort to run away. I also noticed several Cape pigeons and snow petrels flying round the ship and occasionally perching on the rigging.

That night we entered the pack ice in latitude 61° 13' south and longitude 63° 41' east and the *Kista Dan's* voyage now became slow and difficult. There is something rather moving about the way our stubborn little ship forces her way little by little through the ice, like Sisyphus rolling his proverbial stone. She steams ahead slowly and cautiously, lest she should run too hard onto the big floes or the dangerous and treacherous growlers, working ahead until she loses way, then astern, then ahead again, constantly altering course to attack the weakest spots in the pack ice's armor. The ship's bow does all the work in this battle with the ice, and I used to enjoy lingering on the furthest point of the forepeak and leaning right out over the rail, so that I could see just what was happening.

Thin Edge of the World

The *Kista Dan's* bow was specially shaped in a gentle curve just above the water. When she hit small floes or lumps of iceberg she merely brushed them aside without trouble, but when she came upon a more solid mass of ice she slid up onto it like a sled. When the ice was thin she broke it with her own weight, but when it was too thick the ship was jammed in the ice and could go no further. So she went astern and charged the ice again, gradually driving a sort of furrow across the floe, until finally it gave way and broke in pieces, letting the ship subside heavily into her natural element.

Captain Petersen was always at the duplicate controls in the crow's nest. The bridge was often deserted, and the ship looked oddly as if she had been left to look after herself. The pack was very thick and, though we sometimes forged ahead through channels of unfrozen water, we did not average more than one or two knots.

That evening Dovers killed a Weddell seal to feed the dogs. The ship stopped so that he and Georges Schwartz could cut it up and bring it aboard. We were then on latitude 66° 32′ south, only one minute of latitude from the Antarctic Circle, which we crossed that night.

For two days the ship went on driving her way through the pack ice, sometimes very thick and closely packed and sometimes strewn with expanses of open water. We passed very near some large flat-topped icebergs and could clearly see their stratification. The weather was still fine and not at all cold. There was no wind and the air was extraordinarily clear. The number of birds and seals had increased, and we had the good luck to spot among the Weddell's and crab-eaters a Ross seal, one of the rarest of antarctic seals. Only about a hundred Ross seals have been recorded, and twenty-nine of them were observed by the *Norsel* expedition.

On February 2 we began to see the mountains of Mac-Robertson Land, two fine rocky ranges running down from the icecap towards the coast. We all were excited to be so near our destination, especially as we were finding more and more open water and seemed to be coming to the end of the pack ice, where we should be able to make better speed. In the afternoon the *Kista Dan* stopped on the edge of an expanse of open water large enough for an airplane to take off on a reconnaissance flight. The ship moored to a large floe, the airplane was cast off from its cradle, the tarpaulin covers were removed, and it was carefully lowered by a special derrick and was soon resting on its floats on the water. Leckie, our Number One Pilot, climbed aboard with Dr. Law, and we watched them taxi away to find a place where they could take off.

Meanwhile, we went over the other side onto the ice floe to stretch our legs. There we were received by a deputation of emperor and Adélie penguins, which stared at us curiously and without fear of our unknown species. Their tameness made it easy to film and photograph them. They are as agile and swift in the water, where they flash past like arrows, as they are slow and awkward on land. This is especially true of the emperors, who walk with a stately waddle, rolling from one foot to the other. When they come out of the sea they leap up, striking the water hard with their short wings, so that they jump out of the sea like a jack-in-the-box.

While we were busy watching these fascinating creatures, the airplane returned from its flight with the news that we should have an easy passage until we came to a barrier of ice, where it would be possible to disembark. But from there to the rocky coast of Mac-Robertson Land, where the base camp was to be established, we should have to carry all the gear on sleds and weasels for about fifteen miles. This might be a very difficult task, for we should have to cross black ice, which looked more like young and probably rather weak sea ice than old ice, which would have been white and covered with patches of snow. Bob Dovers was getting ready to make a second reconnaissance to find out more about the state of this ice when the weather changed: snow began to fall and the temperature rose to 42° F. Flying was out of the question.

Through the Ice

The *Kista Dan* cast off her moorings and went on steaming south. The going was easy but somewhat slow, so as not to risk running hard on a reef or a submerged iceberg. But it was not long before we reached a huge sheet of open water as calm as a lake. Although it was now late in the evening there was still daylight in that high southern latitude — a wan and dreary daylight. Heavy clouds hung low in the sky, which shone with an other-worldly light, the temperature was strangely mild, and the air and the sea were perfectly calm and silent as our ship moved slowly and noiselessly on between the fantastic shapes of towering icebergs, standing like dream islands in this nightmarish landscape, which reminded me irresistibly of Böcklin's *Island of the Dead*.

I stood for a long while alone on the foredeck, deeply affected by this inhuman and desolate scene and rejoicing to find solitude again. The supernatural silence all around me seemed almost agonizing, though I could not tell why. I felt as if I were on the brink of a mysterious revelation. A few steps would take me back to the warm and friendly atmosphere down below, but I felt curiously detached from the men on the ship, as if I belonged to the frozen, mineral world around me, as if I had been fused into it and become a part of it. But at last the cold of the night drove me from my long and lonely meditations; I went back to my cabin, tiptoeing through the silent ship so as not to awake my sleeping companions.

When I awoke, I found that the ship had stopped. She was moored to a great floe, on which I saw, through the bay window of our cozy cabin, a group of emperor penguins a few feet away and apparently much interested to see such a strange spectacle. Soon we were on the move again, and before long we had reached the barrier of coastal ice which our plane had flown over the day before. Its undulating edge fell sheer, as if cut with a knife, into the open sea, which seemed almost black among all that whiteness now that the sun was shining once again.

This barrier of ice was alive with Adélie penguins, chattering busily, diving in troops from the ice, swimming, fishing and playing around the ship, darting about with incredible speed and leaving a pattern of silver trails in the dark water. The edge of the barrier seemed to be a meeting-place for all kinds of creatures. Weddell seals sprawled lazily among excited groups of penguins, while skuas, petrels and Cape pigeons wheeled around the *Kista Dan*. A majestic school of whales was going through its grand maneuvers some way off, spouting up columns of moist breath which spread out in plumes of white mist against the deep blue sky.

Through the Ice

The *Kista Dan* cruised slowly along the edge of the barrier, rather as if she were a flagship reviewing this antarctic zoo, though actually she was looking for a flaw in this castle of ice, a breach where she could batter her way in. At noon, having found nothing, she stopped, turned her bow towards the ice and prepared for a frontal attack.

We were now only sixteen miles from Mac-Robertson Land and could see every detail of the two rocky ranges we had sighted on the day before. They looked exasperatingly close, so clearly outlined against the sky — they seemed to be mocking us. For, in fact, those sixteen miles of ice were a more effective barrier than one thousand miles of open water. It would take a long time, at least eight days of hard work and a great many trial attacks and long detours, to cover that miserable little distance.

Icebreaking began again — a slow, monotonous job; and it was discouraging to think of the length of the channel we had to cut through the ice. The *Kista Dan* charged at speed, her bows slid over the ice, crushing it under her weight, gaining twenty to thirty yards before she came to a stop. Then she pulled out astern and charged again with all the force of her fifteen hundred horsepower to gain another thirty yards. So she went on indefatigably, methodically, biting through the dead weight of barrier ice step by step. The track behind us grew longer, but it was still a ludicrously short channel, littered with ice fragments. At midday we halted, having painfully covered a mile.

Bob Dovers was losing patience and decided to see if he could find a landing place on the shore. The airplane was let down onto the ice, this time wearing skis, and flew off towards the coast. On his return, Bob told us that he had found a very fine rocky platform, which seemed to have everything needed for a base. It was easy to approach from the sea as well as accessible to the plateau. But to get there we had to cross fifteen miles of barrier ice, and to carry everything ashore would need so many trips that it would leave the fuel supply dangerously low. Moreover, the ice was too dangerous for the weasels to be able to travel safely with full loads. There was nothing for it but to go on icebreaking. The captain made another reconnaissance to see if he could find a better passage, but the result was depressingly negative. There wasn't one. So we had to go on plowing the furrow we had started.

I was by now quite used to the dull sound of the ship hitting the ice, and it was this familiar noise, accompanied by the Chadburn bell signals and the throbbing of the engines, which awakened me on February 4. Everyone was more or less at a loose end, so most of us spent the day walking about the ice, watching the ship's progress, kicking a football about or amusing ourselves by watching the antics of the Adélie penguins, which during this dreary period provided our chief entertainment.

There was no end to the number of these birds, and the barren gray surface of the immense desert of ice was scored with their little black tracks stretching out of sight. They had come ten or twelve miles from their rookeries on the small rocky islands near the shore in order to reach the edge of the barrier ice, where they could fish and get food for themselves and their young. They waddle along in single file, one behind the other for protection against the wind. From time to time they rest, lying flat on their bellies, and then bravely resume their march, trekking something like twenty-five miles a day in all weathers, even when it blows a blizzard. As soon as they reach the open water they dive in and gambol about, leaping and diving like porpoises, and fishing for those little shellfish called euphausiids. There are so many penguins so closely packed together that the water seethes with them. When they have stopped fishing they leap back onto the ice with astonishing agility, often slipping and skidding as they land. They shake themselves briskly, dripping and glistening in the sun, and then, as calmly as they came, they set out with tiny steps on their long journey back to the family rookery, their stomachs full of good nourishing pap to feed their chicks.

They liked to stay near the ship because they could fish in the channel of open water astern of her, and so shorten their long pilgrimage by several miles. But this morning they were restless, and their frolics in the water were often interrupted by a wild stampede, apparently as a result of some signal which only they understood. Two black dorsal fins, with a wide white band, appeared above the surface from time to time, cutting through the water at a tremendous speed. They belonged to a pair of killer whales, savage brutes which usually prey on whales, but when they cannot get their favorite food they do not spurn such small fry as penguins. A few rifle shots put the killers to flight, soon peace was restored, and the friendly Adélies returned quietly to their fishing.

All this time the icebreaking went on as slowly and laboriously as ever. It is most impressive to stand on the barrier ice nearby and watch the ship's heavy solid hull battering obstinately against the passive ice, tipping up great blocks until they overturn with a crash, and slowly driving a way through the ice field. Sometimes the ice holds her like a vice, and she cannot move. Then we all turn out with whatever weapons we can lay our hands on — shovels, picks, boat hooks, oars, spars — and set to with all our strength to smash the blocks of ice until we have freed the hull.

On February 5 an important decision was made. At five o'clock in the morning the sun was shining brightly and the decks of the *Kista Dan* were humming with activity. Dr. Law and Bob Dovers were tired of waiting and had decided to send a party to the shore to start to work on the base while the ship was on her way. Two parties, the first consisting of Dovers, Schwartz and Macey, the second of Russell and Harvey, were to set out, each in a weasel, towing a sled laden with provisions, tools, clothes and sleeping gear, and a "barge" — a sort of hut-cum-sled which can be used as a workshop, shelter or cookhouse for the base party. We did not take long to unload onto the ice, encouraged by the bright sunshine and a fresh dry frost (21° F.) without a breath of wind. By eleven o'clock the sleds were loaded and coupled to the weasels and the little caravan moved off to the cheers of those of us who stayed behind on the *Kista Dan*. I was most impressed by the way this expedition had been organized. Nothing had been left to chance: every man had worked together to a plan, doing his job with all his heart and with no fuss. There was no vain shouting or argument.

Our ship went on with her thankless task until late at

night, for the sun did not set much before eleven o'clock. The end of this day was very beautiful; the ethereal clarity of the air and the pure starry sky touched me deeply. The mountains of Mac-Robertson Land stood out sharply against the sky, and one could almost count the crevasses in the great glacier which descended from the polar icecap. Little by little the shadow of night spread over the immense plain of ice, which, now that the warmth of daylight had gone, became a lunar landscape, utterly dead and inhuman; but for a long time the slopes of the icecap to the south were still tinged with an extraordinary range of pinks and mauves and blues.

Then the weather changed suddenly, and for two days we were attacked by a ferocious gale blowing at sixty miles per hour. The *Kista Dan* halted her journey through the ice, and began behaving rather curiously, steaming backwards and forwards and rotating slowly on her axis. Thus she eventually managed to break the ice all round her and make a large round pool in which she could maneuver more freely than in her narrow channel. This precaution had been taken because the storm might make the pack ice break up, which would be dangerous to the ship. It might also open channels in the ice, which we had to be ready to make use of, whatever their direction.

Through the Ice

The next morning we were suddenly summoned from our bunks by an order from the captain calling all hands on deck. The ice was breaking up. The force of the wind sweeping irresistibly over the vast bare ice field had opened cracks in the ice, and now huge broken chunks were moving across the sea, threatening to crush any obstacle that stood in their way. Our ship was held in a vice, and huge blocks of ice began to build up slowly and inexorably beside the hull in an enormous pile. We all crowded onto the deck armed with sticks and spars ready to push overboard any blocks which threatened to fall in on us. Fortunately there was no need for us, because the pile of ice stopped advancing at the level of the deck. No ordinary ship could have withstood this terrific pressure, but our gallant *Kista Dan*, with her reinforced hull and her curved lines, stood up to the assault without flinching, at least so we thought, but when we got back into open water the captain found that one of the plates at the waterline had begun to start.

The ice pack now looked very striking and strange. The old flat and unbroken surface had turned into a vast plowed field, contorted by the storm and looking as if there had been an earthquake. Long sinuous lines of broken floes were tangled round the ship, their rims clashed together, and they rode up one on top of the other until they formed top-heavy piles of tottering blocks. Between these chaotic heaps strips of open water appeared, showing us a way out of our trap. The wind blew as hard as ever, the sky was gray and low, it was bitterly cold, and it was no fun trying to hold a camera in such weather. As soon as I had finished taking photographs on the empty deck I hurried down to the warm shelter of my cabin.

The cabins on the *Kista Dan* were very pleasant and comfortable. I shared mine with Bob Dovers and Bruce Stinear, our geologist, and it was positively roomy compared with the usual tiny boxes on merchant ships. Besides the bunks, there was a sofa, a largish table, a washbasin, capacious drawers and well-fitted cupboards. But what I liked most about it was that instead of the usual tiny round porthole there was a large bay filling the whole of the outer side of the cabin, with two large windows, giving us a wide view of the outside world. The windows were made of thick glass and were absolutely weatherproof, but by an ingenious and effective device they could be opened wide when the weather was fine, the sea calm and the cold bearable. Thus, without leaving our cabin, we could enjoy the pure outside air, the brightness and warmth of the sun and a splendid uninterrupted view of the ice field. A powerful system of electric heating kept the cabin agreeably warm, however cold it might be outside.

Through the Ice

Although our cabin was so comfortable, we might not have been able to live amicably together at such close quarters had it not been for my companions' British reserve. Their attitude was perfectly suited to my taste for solitude and to my natural dislike of prying into my neighbors' lives or having them pry into mine.

I have had too much experience of having to live with other people on sea or land, in various parts of the world, not to know all its disadvantages, and I have already said a good deal on the subject. But until I came on this expedition I had never chanced to live with such discreet and tactful companions, and I must admit that for once a communal life was almost better than a solitary one, for human warmth mitigates the chill austerity of solitude, which sometimes tends to dry up a man's heart. The atmosphere reminded me a little of the religious order at Cîteaux, though outwardly and spiritually it was very different: I was able to enjoy solitude as well as company, for we all respected the privacy of one another's own personal life. On the *Kista Dan* our triple cell was often so silent that we each felt as undisturbed as if we were quite alone. We were men whose characters had been formed in the same way, and we were all bent on the same object. It was good to feel one another's silent and tactful sympathy, which did not remain unspoken when the occasion arose. None of this affected our general good humor. Silence could be had for the asking, but it was often interrupted by keen discussions or friends bursting in to tell us some good news or merely anxious to relax outside their own cabins. This made the atmosphere on the boat very friendly and pleasant.

Next day, February 8, the weather was fine again. At breakfast I was surprised to see Bob Dovers, who had been brought back by airplane and was able to tell us what had happened to his reconnaissance party. The treacherous new ice had made the journey difficult and dangerous, and on the first day one of the weasels went through the ice and fell into the water. Luckily it was the amphibian, and Dovers said they hoped soon to be able to lift it back onto the ice. The remaining weasel towed both the sled and the barge, and the two teams eventually managed to reach a little rocky island near the coast, where they camped to wait until the ice was strong enough for them to get to the site for the base on the mainland. After a good breakfast Bob went off in the airplane to rejoin his party with some extra gear for the camp.

Meanwhile a large sheet of open water had appeared astern of the *Kista Dan*. Her stern lay in the water, but the rest of her hull had been hoisted up by the storm and was sitting on a cradle of ice, while huge blocks were jammed against her sides. The churning propeller was powerless to haul her astern off the ice. It needed two days of hard work before we got her free. We used every possible means, even the most drastic, detonating explosive charges to blow up the pack ice, and putting out ice anchors and hauling on them with the winch; but the explosives made only small cracks, because the ice was so elastic, and the anchors were always dragging. In the end we found we got the best results by the absurdly primitive method of smashing the ice by hand with boat hooks and spikes and shoving it back out of the way. We all worked like an industrious army of ants — each individual effort was puny, but together we shifted mountains — and by ten o'clock on the morning of February 10 the ship was under way again, steaming through loose pack ice and skirting the ice field on our west.

We were now only nine miles from the coast (latitude 67° 20′ south, longitude 63° 10′ east), and ahead of us the bare black cone of Welch Island showed we were nearly there. The airplane had just reconnoitered a channel which looked practicable, and we entered it, after rounding a little ice-covered island. The weather was perfect, the temperature was 25° F. and the sun shone in all its brilliance. The air was wonderfully clear, and in this pure light the scene looked quite astonishingly beautiful: there was the ice-clad island just astern and the long, winding channel ahead, with its icy shores swarming with Adélie penguins, and, very close now, the mountains of Mac-Robertson Land.

But in the antarctic it is a mistake to rejoice too soon and surprises are more likely to be nasty than pleasant. At two o'clock in the afternoon the *Kista Dan* was trapped in the ice once more, and we spent all the rest of that day getting her out again. It was just the same as before: we began by doing all the proper things with explosives and ice anchors, with no result, and finished up hacking her out by hand. It reminded me of the curiously effective methods I had often seen used in the Far East, where thousands of coolies scrape up the earth with their hands and carry it in little baskets on their heads until they succeed in carving motor roads through mountains — a triumph of human patience and determination over the latest mechanical methods.

February 12 was a red-letter day in the history of our expedition. At eight o'clock we were once more under way, still following our narrow winding channel; but, to avoid being trapped again, the *Kista Dan* tacked her way forward, smashing alternate chunks out of the walls of ice to port and starboard. This slowed us down, but we could not have gone fast anyway because we did not know what the bottom was like, and the sailing directions said that the area was full of rocks. The weather had taken a turn for the worse again; it was gloomy and gray, with a savage wind which made it hard to bear the bitter temperature at 16° F.

At about ten o'clock our channel came to an end after leading us through a wilderness of shattered pack ice and large floes. We had reached open sea again, but the ship felt her way forward only very gingerly. Little by little the weather cleared, until the sun was shining in a cloudless blue sky, and its pure rays lit up a strange world of large icebergs and small rocky islands patchily covered with ice, which our ship seemed to be passing in review. But the wind blew as hard as ever, and it was bitterly cold.

At noon the *Kista Dan* stopped a few cables' lengths from Pila Island, a dark, squat mass of rock. We were now six miles southwest of Welch Island and only three miles from the coast, but the pack ice was thicker in that direction and blocked our path. It seemed as if we had come down a blind alley. So the ship turned back and went round the north of Welch Island and a whole string of smaller islands. Our passage towards the east, sometimes in clear water and sometimes through the middle of the pack, was very beautiful, for we were cruising very near the coast and could see every detail of the cliffs of ice and the icebergs that broke off from them. I took a lot of films and photographs, but the cold was cruel, and I had to keep going down below to warm my frozen hands.

We then turned and followed another string of islands running southwards towards the coast until we ran into a thick and solid ice field, which slowed us down again. At six o'clock a weasel appeared on the ice and approached us, following a trail of little red flags. It kept out of the ship's way as she still forged slowly ahead. The two men waved to us to stop, and as the weasel came nearer we recognized Dovers and Schwartz, who had come to welcome us. The sun had gone, a strong wind was blowing and there was a black frost, so they lost no time in coming aboard, and we fell into each others' arms much moved, though unwilling to show it. Stanley and Livingstone transferred to the antarctic, I thought, as we went down to celebrate the happy meeting.

During dinner Bob and Georges told us all their adventures: the amphibian weasel falling into the sea and Bob and Macey skipping out on the ice like Adélies, and pitching camp on an island among a rookery of penguins. Then they salvaged the weasel with a windlass Bob had taken there by plane, using a method which I was soon to see and use myself. Finally they reached the shore, after a very tricky journey towing the sled and the barge over treacherous ice, and began setting up the base camp on a great rocky platform, which seemed to be the best available site.

The rocky islands all around us looked very grim with their great slabs of brown stone, glistening with ice and without the smallest plant on them anywhere. The mountains of Mac-Robertson Land looked equally forbidding through the field glasses. The rock with its armor of ice and the jagged snow-clad ridges could hardly have been more discouraging to the mountaineer on that bitter evening.

We were now very near our goal. Dovers and Schwartz soon left us to go back to their party, bravely refusing the bourgeois comfort of the ship to which they no longer belonged. Then the ship got under way again, gradually forcing her way through the thinner ice to get as near the camp as possible. It was not far off now, and we could already see the red shapes of the weasels and the barge hardly one hundred yards away. The voyage out was over. It had taken sixteen days from Kerguelen — they had been busy, difficult days, full of hard work and discomfort, but they had never been dull. I had enjoyed all sorts of new and exciting experiences in one of the most wonderful and impressive places on earth.

CHAPTER NINE

The Birth of a Base

THE antarctic continent gave us a somewhat chilly reception, and our first impressions of Mac-Robertson Land were not encouraging. It seemed to be going to test our powers of endurance once more. Throughout the night the wind had blown a gale, and in the morning it reached a speed of ninety miles per hour; so, what with the wind and the summery temperature of 13° F., I was not tempted to smoke my pipe on deck.

But this was a small inconvenience, only to be expected in this part of the world, and the storm caused far more serious harm. One of the airplanes, though firmly lashed down on deck, was so seriously damaged, with a warped fuselage and a buckled wing, that it was unlikely it could be repaired, and for future reconnaissances we should have to rely on the remaining aircraft, which fortunately was safe in the hold. For the moment we could do nothing; there was no point in worrying about repairing the aircraft or landing stores, so we all stayed put — the ship's company in their cabins and

The Birth of a Base

the landing party in their barges. There was not a sign
of life from anybody, which made the dead world outside seem more desolate than ever, and the vast polar
silence was broken only by the howling of the wind
and the strange, hoarse, stifled voices of the sled dogs
fighting in their narrow cages. For huskies, as their name
may suggest, do not bark, but only utter an odd throaty
wail.

In the afternoon Bob and Schwartz came on board to
arrange the landing program with Dr. Law. They were
very disappointed at the weather at their future base,
which was almost as vile as at Port Martin, in Adélie
Land, where they had both wintered. The wind was almost constant, for it was a "catabatic wind," which
comes down in squalls from the polar plateau and is
caused by the difference in temperature between the
plateau and the coast, being particularly violent at sun-
rise and sunset. It would make it very difficult to put up
the prefabricated huts for the base and promised bitter
blizzards for the winter.

Bob had also noticed during his first reconnaissance
that there were no penguin rookeries on the mainland;
they were all on little islands a few miles from the coast.
This was a sign of a difference in climate. The islands
were outside the range of the catabatic winds, and the
penguins had learned from instinct and experience to

choose the best site for their rookeries. Men are less intelligent. We had been worrying about all sorts of things which the penquins had blithely ignored. We had to suffer the climate on the mainland in order to set up our huts on better platforms and be able to reach the polar plateau with our weasels.

Schwartz was very concerned about food for the dogs. We had brought a supply of special tinned pemmican for them, but these rations were intended for sled expeditions; normally they were to be fed on meat. But there did not seem to be many seals about; Georges had recently gone off in a weasel to look for them, but he had seen only six. To keep the twenty-five dogs going through the winter (two of them had already died) he had to stock up with at least seventy or eighty seals before the weather became so bad that hunting was impossible. Otherwise he would have to reduce the pack to twenty, keeping the best animals and killing off the others, for the Australian law did not allow us to take them back to Melbourne. This would have been an absolute tragedy for poor Schwartz, who loved his dogs like children. But there was still time, and we decided to wait before doing anything drastic. The god of dogs (if not the god of seals) would no doubt help us to find enough for these luckless creatures to justify our optimism and prevent Georges having to make a Cornelian choice.

The Birth of a Base

Meanwhile the wind dropped. Bob and Schwartz went back to the base, towing the dogs' kennels behind their weasel. We should start unloading next day, weather permitting, and Dr. Law called us all together to work out a detailed plan of campaign so that everyone knew exactly what to do.

February 13 turned out to be one of the finest days of our stay in Mac-Robertson Land. The wind had gradually abated to about twenty-five miles per hour, which made it quite easy to bear the temperature of 23° F. The sky was clear and the sun shone brightly, and unloading went ahead well, although our teamwork was not yet properly co-ordinated. It got better during the ten days it took to finish the job, which was made much easier because the ship was surrounded by ice. The sled could lie alongside and be loaded directly from the ship's derricks, just as if we were berthed against a quay. The weasels then towed the loaded sled about one hundred yards to the base.

The route was fairly easy, for the rocky platform was not at all far above the ice. There was, it is true, a series of crevasses between the fixed land ice and the tidal pack ice, but a safe route had been staked out which the weasels could follow without much danger right up to the platform, towing their sleds to the unloading point.

But the pack ice was weak in places, and this caused several accidents. On the very first day one of the weasels broke through the ice and fell into the water, in spite of the carefully marked route. Luckily it was the amphibian again. It had already been in trouble during the first reconnaissance and seemed naturally prone to such accidents. We now knew just how to haul it out, and I was interested to lend a hand and see how it was done. About twenty yards ahead of the weasel you cut a hole right through the ice with an ice axe. It has to be large enough to take a wooden balk with a strong rope strap fastened to the middle. You push this balk right through the hole until it can turn over sideways under the pack ice and is thus firmly anchored. A block and tackle is hooked on to the rope and connected to a wire cable attached to the front of the weasel. The weasel's motor is then started, and at the same time you haul on the tackle. When the weasel's tracks begin to bite into the ice, wooden planks are put under them to prevent them from skidding on the edge of the ice. The combined efforts of the motor and the tackle soon have the weasel back on the ice again. It all happens very quickly — in little more time than I have taken to describe it.

The site for the base was excellently chosen in everything but climate. The surroundings were very beautiful and it was conveniently accessible and well fitted for building on. It lay at the head of a sheltered little bay, which we named Horseshoe Harbor because of its shape. The *Kista Dan* lay in the ice in the center of this bay, and from the upper deck one could enjoy a splendid panoramic view of the whole scene through the clear sunny air.

In the foreground, not one hundred yards away, a brownish strip ran along the shore, with the red weasels and barges and heaps of cases and unloaded gear marking the site of the camp. It consisted of a series of rocky terraces rising gently from the level of the pack ice to the top of the moraine. The highest terrace formed a great platform protected by a vertical wall of rock. It was well sheltered, and the nature of the ground would be a great help in building the main hut. It was cut off from the south by a high moraine of screes and jumbled blocks of stone, separating the camp from the snout of a great glacier creeping down from the icecap and ending suddenly in a high sheer cliff of splintering ice.

Towards the east, along the curving coastline, I could see a rocky headland marking the entrance to the bay, and behind it another small cove where the snout of another glacier met the sea. The western headland pointed towards the string of small islands which we had followed on our way here and which closed the bay on this side. Finally, behind this headland, the coast stretched away in one straight line of high even cliffs of ice, with only very few peaks of rock.

After a while I got tired of standing motionless on the deck and decided to stretch my legs. I went ashore and immediately started to walk up to the crest of the moraine, after which I explored the rocky peninsula to the west of the camp. The islands are linked together by the frozen sea, and it is very easy to walk from one to another. From the western side of these islets one cannot see the camp or ship, and it is a most exalting feeling to be utterly alone in this untouched world of ice, without a sign of man or any living creature, as silent as a star.

I felt drunk with solitude, which was none the less real because I was so close to the ship and the camp, and could have seen them merely by sticking my head over the rocks. There was not even the excitement of having to suffer antarctic cold. There were not more than fourteen degrees of frost, with not a breath of wind, and the sun beat down strongly through the pure dry air, so that I actually felt the heat and had to take off my sweater, which left me in the jacket and duck trousers which I usually wore in summer in Kerguelen. I also took off my gloves, which were quite unnecessary and got in the way when I was taking photographs.

Poor Schwartz was suffering from a severe relapse of

the lumbago he had contracted when he was in Adélie Land. He was unable to do any hard work and came with me on my little explorations round the base. Although my first excursion had been so comfortably easy, the sense of security was quite false. The most innocent walk can be turned into a grim adventure by a change of weather, a crevasse, an avalanche of ice or any ordinary accident occurring at some distance from the base. Georges, who spoke from experience, advised me very strongly against these solitary outings, which have always attracted me so much.

On February 14, in splendid weather, Georges and I went off to explore beyond the headland to the east of our base. After crossing a moraine of enormous blocks of red rock, we reached a little frozen bay. We had some trouble crossing the ice, which was full of crevasses and very slippery, and our Vibram soles gave us a poor footing; but finally we reached a small island surrounded by a whole squadron of great flat-topped icebergs which had broken off from a gigantic glacier that flowed steeply down from the polar plateau to the frozen sea. It seemed as though the icebergs were lying at anchor in this natural roadstead, waiting for the spring thaw to break away and drift towards the warmer waters. I took the opportunity to collect specimens of different kinds of mosses and lichens which grow in the damp hollows and sheltered corners of the rocks. I was surprised to find such a variety of plants, and by the brilliant colors — red, yellow and green — of certain lichens, which cling so firmly to the rocks that it is hard to pull them off.

There were few birds, except the skuas, which had been flocking round since we began unloading and settled in great numbers around the ship and the kennels, where they found a varied and unexpected diet. In retaliation the cook used to shoot a few of them every day, for, although they look so unattractive and live by scavenging, they are the most eatable of the polar birds. Their breasts, when carefully removed and skillfully cooked, made an excellent imitation *tournedos* much appreciated by most of the party. I was one of the few who could not stand this sort of food and infinitely preferred the cheese, cereals and canned fruits from the ship's storeroom.

The antarctic skuas are quite different from those in Kerguelen and belong to another species: MacCormick's skua. They are larger and their plumage is a lighter beige, with broad white bars on the wings. Besides the skuas one sees a few snow petrels around the base. These delightful birds are white all over, with black beaks and dark gray feet. They had hatched their eggs shortly before we came, and as we slid down the steep rocks we often came upon young birds still in their nests. They had the curious habit, which I had often seen in Kerguelen, of spitting at intruders with a jet of thick and sticky red saliva.

Our second outing had a more serious purpose, for Schwartz had to set about finding some seals to feed his dogs. We crossed the rocky peninsula that I had explored alone and reached the pack ice at the foot of the ice cliff to the west of our camp. This immense ice wall, about one hundred and fifty feet high, sometimes sheer and sometimes overhanging, was a most magnificent sight. Its face was deeply scored from top to bottom with perpendicular cracks dividing the surface into pillars, like the columns of a cathedral. Some of them had slipped and were propped against the wall like flying buttresses of crystal, others had broken off and lay in huge blocks at the foot of the cliff, warning one not to come too near the cliff. But in any case the way was usually barred by great crevasses like the *rimayes* on glaciers in the Alps. Today we were wearing crampons and felt much more sure on our feet, so our old mountaineering instincts came out and we made several short climbs across the ice, and eventually reached the plateau by following the easiest way up the cliff.

But none of this had helped us to find any seals, so we had to leave the cliff to get on with more serious business. We had some difficulty in reaching the sea ice because our climb had taken us into a maze of crevasses, and in order to get out we had to do some serious ice work, which reminded me of good old days above Chamonix. When we were on level ground again we were able to move at a good pace along the base of the ice cliffs.

From a distance the coast looks quite straight, but actually it is very complicated, consisting of the snouts of glaciers between spurs of different sizes. In fact the coastline was so broken that we could not see far ahead, and we were surprised to come upon a large number of crab-eating seals congregating in gaps in the ice cliff and on the sheltered patches of pack ice between the islands. Schwartz had missed them when he was out in the weasel, for he had been too far from the coast and had not explored all the bends in the cliff. Now his heart rejoiced to see such a fine supply of meat for his beloved dogs, and he decided to come back soon with his butcher's tools and vehicles to carry off the booty. Meanwhile the meat supply slept peaceably, sprawling on the ice and basking in the sun without an inkling of the fate, glorious perhaps, but hardly enviable, which awaited them. And so, in this corner of a virgin land, man's first act was to slaughter the innocent inhabitants.

The Birth of a Base

We discussed the rights and wrongs of this ugly business without coming to any conclusion except that since we had brought our dogs so far it was up to us to keep them fed, and soon we came to a large bay with a small rocky island at the entrance. From the top of this rock we had a very fine view of Mount David, one of the three conspicuous peaks in Mac-Robertson Land. We had a clear view because the snout of the glacier reaches right down to the sea instead of breaking off in a high cliff. It was not an attractive mountain, and its slabs of black rock, smooth and coated with sleet, looked abominably difficult to climb.

As soon as we got back Georges went off to feed his dogs and no doubt to tell them in his own way the good news that he had found an unexpected supply of food large enough to feed them all. When they were landed, the dogs were all put out on a great rocky platform partly covered with hard snow, each tethered to the rock by a long chain at some distance from his neighbor. Thus they could move about comfortably and lie on the snow when they were too hot or were thirsty. Visiting this open-air kennel is one of the chief entertainments for the expedition and the ship's company. The dogs are very affectionate and like showing it, but their great size and strength make them rather rough with their friends; and the seal fat rubbed into their fur gives them a strong smell which hardly suits such decorative and much-photographed animals.

It was a striking, if lurid and unappetizing, spectacle to see Georges Schwartz using a hatchet to dismember the carcasses of the great heap of frozen seals not far from the kennels. They keep perfectly fresh in this natural open-air refrigerator, which is infested with skuas keeping a constant watch, waiting for the dogs' feeding time, when they dart in for their own share, in spite of the gunshots that thin their ranks from time to time.

Our base was now officially established and named Mawson, after the great Australian explorer. Before the christening ceremony we had to send an official radio message to Melbourne to get the authority of the Australian Government, and also of course of Professor Sir Douglas Mawson, who lives in retirement in his estate near Sydney.

At the appointed hour all the members of the expedition, who were still living on the ship, drove up in weasels, and the whole Australian team gathered round a flagstaff that had been erected alongside one of the barges of the temporary camp. Dr. Law gave a short address and then, in dead silence, hoisted the Australian flag, while the little group sang "God Save the Queen." We took photographs and films of this historic occasion, the inauguration of the first permanent Australian base on the antarctic continent, and then we all went back to work. I found this simple little ceremony very moving. Everyone was in working clothes, and each one had worked hard and uncomplainingly, in spite of the long hours, often monotonous and discouraging, which they had spent with no thought but to get the job done.

And all the while the summer sun blazed from a pure, blue antarctic sky. The air was still and the glistening ice cliffs around this little corner of the frozen continent lent beauty and splendor to the ceremony.

On the afternoon of February 17 we finished unloading. It had been done in record time, thanks to everyone's strenuous work and also to the unusually fine weather we had had almost all the time. Bob fetched the rest of his things from our cabin, but Stinear was in no hurry to leave the comfort of the ship and stayed on board until the day before she sailed. For she had still to stay a few more days at Mawson until the winter quarters were far enough advanced for the land team to be able to carry on with their routine work as soon as we left.

The base had already made good progress. Building had been going on steadily from the first day, at the same time as the unloading. Two huts were nearly finished; and only their ingenious design had made this possible. The first was a box-shaped building twenty-four feet long, twelve feet broad and eight feet high. It was made entirely of large panels of Duralumin, two layers with heat-insulating material in between. It contained, besides the entrance chamber, Dovers's office, which served also as a geophysical laboratory, the hospital, a large room for meteorological and radio work and a darkroom.

It had been admirably designed and manufactured with remarkable precision. The joints between the panels had been very carefully made, and when they were put together — a quick and easy job — they were quite impervious to air and water. The doors and windows were particularly well designed, and there were emergency exits in case the usual doors were completely snowed in. This great box with its flat roof and its armor of Duralumin, glittering in the sunshine, looked like a huge refrigerator, which is not surprising because it was built on the same principles by a large Australian firm that specializes in cold chambers and freezing apparatus.

The second building to be finished was the provision store. It was the same size as the first building, and put together in just the same way, except that it had double walls, heat-insulated in the usual way. These buildings went up easily and quickly, without snags. This, like everything else, was the result of very careful preparation.

The Birth of a Base

I know of one expedition whose prefabricated buildings turned out to be useless when the time came to as-
semble them. The panels were not all the same size and
could not be fitted together. It was a most unpleasant
situation, ludicrous but quite irremediable, for it was
not discovered until the expedition reached its destination, on the other side of the world, where they could not
possibly get in touch with the makers. This could not
have happened at Mawson as, before the expedition
left Australia, each building had been assembled and
then taken to pieces by the same team that would have
to do the job in the antarctic, supervised by the men
who had made them. This was why everything went so
quickly, without a hitch.

The only difficult work, and that which took most
time, was building the wooden platforms on which the
buildings rested. They were laid on a rock foundation,
and the many almost level expanses at Mawson made it
quite easy to build a wooden frame and chock it up
level with slabs of rock. The frame was then fastened to
the ground by iron clamps driven into the rock, a
wooden floor was nailed down onto it, and the prefabricated panels were assembled on top.

The second storehouse was soon complete and we
could now tidy away the heap of cases and gear which
had already been sorted out ready for stowing. A third

building, still larger than the others, was being erected and its wooden foundation had already been laid. It was designed to house the electric generators and also to be used as a workshop and for shower baths. It was built in the usual way, but a block of concrete had to be set into the foundations so that the two diesel motors for the generators could be firmly bolted down.

The scientific work had already begun. Meteorological observations were being taken regularly and could be sent off now that the radio station was working. A meteorological station had been set up outside the camp on an exposed terrace of rock. It contained the usual instruments: thermometers and barometers, a maximum and minimum thermometer, a hygrometer, various kinds of wind gauges and so forth.

There was still one more storehouse to be set up, and also, of course, the great living hut for the winter party. This was the only piece of the camp which had not been specially made for the ANARE to their own plans, for this hut had been presented to the Australians by the Anglo-Swedish-Norwegian "Norsel" expedition, and since funds were by no means plentiful this generous gift was most welcome. Its construction was solid, and had already passed the test of the antartic. It consisted of a large, square chamber twenty-six feet by twenty-six feet, with a double steeply sloping roof — the only one of its kind, all the others having flat or gently sloping roofs. The walls were double and very well insulated. Inside there were ten identical compartments for the ten members of the team, five on each side of the common room, which was to be a meeting-and-recreation room as well as the dining room and kitchen with a large Aga cooker. In the front of the hut there was an entrance lobby, a meteorological room in which the static anemometer would be kept and, finally, a toilet. It was a handsome building, with its floor covered with a warm red sponge-rubber carpet. The furniture was light in color and practical in design; the chairs and armchairs were comfortable, made of metal tubes and upholstered in royal blue, and everything was designed to please the eye and lighten the life of ten men cloistered together through the long months of polar night. This attention to detail showed a keen sense of the psychology of *homo antarcticus*.

Until this large living hut could be set up, the ten members of the winter party decided to live temporarily in the Duralumin laboratory, where men and their gear were all jumbled together. There were heaps of bedding in the future hospital, which was being used as a dormitory. Dovers's office overflowed with apparatus which had been put there out of the way. Radio and meteorological equipment was stuffed in a corner of a room that was supposed to contain nothing else, the rest of the room being used as a common room, dining room and kitchen. A large hot plate, heated by bottled propane gas, had been installed, and Gleadell, a skillful and stout-hearted cook, who always appeared unruffled and met the worst disasters with a smile, bustled around amid heaps of saucepans, crockery and tinned food, somehow managing to produce delicious meals in spite of the confusion.

Meanwhile the airmen and mechanics had not been wasting their time. Down in the 'tween-decks, out of the wind, they had completely dismantled the airplane that had been damaged by the storm; they had replaced the faulty parts with one of the wings and part of the fuselage from the reserve plane crated in the hold, and by much clever and painstaking patchwork had at last managed to concoct an entirely new airplane. They had flown it on test flights over Mac-Robertson, Kemp and Enderby Lands, and had taken reconnaissance photographs.

The *Kista Dan* also had been preparing to sail. She had had a hard time getting free of the ice in which she had been imprisoned since her arrival, but she had now made an exploratory trip to the east. Going back by the way she had come, she had reached Welch Island without much difficulty. The water ahead seemed fairly open, and this was confirmed by the airmen. We could now be on our way.

The next stage of our voyage, towards Princess Elizabeth Land, promised to be an exciting adventure in a new and certainly very beautiful country, but it would be the end of a congenial piece of teamwork, and would break up a happy and united group. The men whom I was going to leave behind, especially Georges Schwartz, were my very good friends, and I should be sorry to say good-by.

I had often admired their courage, endurance and good humor and appreciated the kindness and consideration to me, a foreigner who did not belong to their expedition, but whom they had adopted as one of themselves. Their tact and consideration and their typical British respect for their neighbor's privacy, especially when he wishes to be alone or to be quiet, made it easy for me to bear — and indeed enjoy — the inevitable drawbacks of being confined on a ship with other men.

I had no less admiration for their team spirit, and appreciated the pleasant atmosphere which it created. The small number of men, all scientists and technicians, without any menials to do the dirty work, meant that everyone had to turn to and take his share, not only in his own particular work, which was often unpleasant enough in the antarctic weather, but also in unloading, building, maintenance, cleaning and other tasks by no means pleasant for people who are not accustomed to them. And all this was done good-humoredly, without grumbling. While we were unloading, the work was particularly hard, and occasional spells of bad weather made the long days seem longer. To begin with, the work did not flow too smoothly, and there was plenty of matter for criticism or spiteful remarks. But neither Schwartz nor I ever heard a single complaint or noticed any sign of ill temper.

I could not help admiring such excellent discipline, such affectionate loyalty to the leader of the expedition, such understanding of this difficult task and appreciation of the inevitable flaws in so large an organization. I was in a good position to appreciate it after having spent a year in another mission, but I do not want to make invidious comparisons. The two missions were hardly comparable. One was a small, well-knit team of scientists with a single object: to create something that had not existed before — to set up a scientific station on the antarctic continent, in an extraordinary climate and very difficult conditions, a new project in which all Australia was interested. The other was a large permanent base, which had been going for several years, running in much the same humdrum regular way as a factory or an administrative office, well built, comfortable, in a bleak

The Birth of a Base

but not impossible climate, with a large and varied personnel.

On February 22 the base was far enough advanced for us to leave the winter party to their own devices. Our departure was fixed for the next day, everyone was feverishly busy with final arrangements, but the most overworked man in the station was certainly the officer in charge of the post office. For several days the poor fellow had spent his days and part of his nights in stamping masses of letters and stowing them in bags in the saloon. I would never have believed twenty men capable of writing so many letters and post cards. I afterwards discovered that there were more than thirty thousand of them.

This immense spate of correspondence was due to the fact that an official post office had been opened at Mawson and that the first stamped mail from this new station would be of great interest and value to stamp collectors, although the stamps were only ordinary Australian stamps, overprinted MAWSON — ANTARCTICA. Next year the station would have stamps of its own. While I was helping Bill Storer, the good-natured meteorologist who had assumed the duties of postmaster, I noticed that packets containing several hundred stamped cards, some of them specially printed for the occasion, were addressed to the same address, generally that of a stamp dealer. I must say I was shocked to see the way the mission was being commercially exploited. On the other hand, I was delighted and rather touched to see that Registered Letter No. 1 signed by all the Australian members of the expedition, was addressed to Her Majesty the Queen, Buckingham Palace, London.

For the last day the members of the winter party had the run of the ship, and they took advantage of this to finish their correspondence and to wallow in the ship's bathroom while they still had the chance. The ship party, on the other hand, was very busy tidying up the ship and the cabins, arranging and stowing the rest of the cargo in the holds, making all sorts of preparations for getting under way, lashing down the airplane on the quarter-deck and thinking up entertainments for the party that night. Luckily we had splendid weather, warm and windless — the sun temperature reached 58° F. at two o'clock, when it was 22° F. in the shade.

In the evening we all met together for a final dinner and celebration. It was a gay evening, and songs and laughter hid the emotion which most of us felt. Dr. Law accompanied the old traditional Australian and Danish songs with his accordion, and Frank Morgan, the aircraft mechanic, played his fiddle. We also sang a certain French song, no less traditional, which had been learned during the visit to Kerguelen. The champagne which had been presented by the quartermaster of the French mission added a note of French gaiety to the enthusiasm inspired by the Australians' punch and whisky and the Danes' aquavit, pleasantly symbolizing the collaboration of the three countries in the success of the expedition.

It was late. There was much to do on the next day, and we were due to start early, but the Australians could not leave before we had sung "For He's a Jolly Good Fellow" for the benefit of Dr. Law. When this solemn rite was over we went to our bunks for the last night in Mac-Robertson Land.

CHAPTER TEN

Off to Princess Elizabeth Land

AT six o'clock on February 23, Dr. Law was the first up. He went round all the cabins waking the sleepers, and soon the ten members of the antarctic party came on board. The last letters were handed in, the last messages given and the last farewells said. After singing "For He's a Jolly Good Fellow" once more, the whole winter party went back onto the ice to wait for the ship to sail, which was due to happen at half past six. The sun was already high, but a piercing wind was blowing and it was bitterly cold (25° F.).

Everyone, whether on deck or on the ice, was stamping his feet and rubbing his hands to keep warm and wishing in his heart that these distressing good-bys were over. It is always the same story when the last good-bys have been said in railway stations or at the dock. The parting friends have nothing more to say and stand gazing at one another with silly smiles on their faces, thinking that it is about time the train or the boat started moving. But our ship was even more unwilling to start than most; she seemed utterly stuck, and at last the antarctic party, frozen to the marrow and tired of stamping on the ice in the bitter wind, threw us a quick "bye-bye" and hurried off to the shelter of their huts.

Four hours later the *Kista Dan* was still there. All her engines were throbbing, but she had not moved an inch. Should we have to spend the winter there? The usual drill began. Ice anchors were put out and hauled in on the winch, the hull was freed of ice, explosives were detonated . . . and finally at a quarter past eleven she began to move. The siren blew and the ten men on the shore came hurrying up, clinging together on the top of the open weasel, and followed us for a few hundred yards. We took our final photos and waved our last good-bys. Soon the weasel and its passengers and then the huts of the base camp faded in the distance, and we were left alone to gaze at the mountain ranges and glaciers of Mac-Robertson Land glistening in the translucent air. The second lap of our voyage had begun.

Our first object was to explore and chart the eastern coast of Mac-Robertson Land. Our observations from the ships were to be completed by air reconnaissances over the interior. We then proposed to land on the west coast of the MacKenzie Sea and to explore Cape Amery and Sandefjord Bay. After that the *Kista Dan* was to make for the Vestfold Hills on the Ingrid Christensen coast in Princess Elizabeth Land. There we should try to land and set up a triangulation point, completing our observations by air reconnaissances and air photographs.

After leaving Horseshoe Harbor we reached the open sea near Welch Island at about half past one. There we turned and headed east. The ship followed the coastline a few miles out to sea and steamed slowly through indescribably lovely scenery. The little rocky islands and the great flat-topped icebergs were outlined against the pure blue sky, and in the background we could see the gleaming slopes of the glaciers of Mac-Robertson Land. We had no difficulty in keeping up a regular speed of four knots, sometimes through open water and sometimes through loose pack ice formed of large floes and beautifully shaped pancakes which oscillated gently with the swell and made the sea look as if it were covered with gigantic white water lilies. These pancakes are formed by the sea freezing. They are large discs of one to three feet in diameter and not more than four inches thick. Their edges are turned up slightly, which makes them look particularly like real pancakes. Later they freeze together to form pack ice.

Towards evening the sky began to cloud over just as we turned south and headed for the Scullin Monolith. We hoped to reach this landmark on the following day, but suddenly the weather worsened and held us up for some time. It grew very cold and the sea began to be covered with all kinds of new ice — fine greasy "slush," thicker gritty "sludge" and newly formed pancakes. The sea was rising hourly and a very heavy swell was battering the ship. The sight of the enormous waves, entirely covered with a skin of ice, smashing on the deck and showering the ship with splinters of ice was most impressive, but there were few of us to admire it and the tables in the dining saloon were empty. After twenty-four hours of this rough handling we anchored a few cables' lengths from the Monolith. The swell was not quite so bad as it had been, but the weather was as hostile as ever and the dark rocks on the coast kept appearing and then vanishing in the mist in a very grim manner. The screaming cries of clouds of sea birds wheeling round the ship only added to the desolation.

The high pyramid of the Scullin Monolith is one of the few rocky landmarks. It is almost a resort for pilgrims, for Mawson, Rayner and Lars Christensen have all landed there, and now Dr. Law hoped to follow their example. During the 25th the weather cleared a little, and by the light of a few feeble rays of sunshine we were able to see where we were. The high rocky slopes of the Monolith were completely covered by rookeries of petrels and Adélie penguins. One could pick out every bird; they looked like thousands of little black dots spread out all over the screes of shale or crowded on the bank of ice at the foot of the rock.

We intended to land here to leave a dump of provisions and camping gear for reconnaissance parties from the Mawson team, so in spite of the abominable weather the motorboat was launched and set off for the coast with Dr. Law, Dr. Gwynn, Jim Brookes and Dick Thomson on board. We watched them anxiously as the swell, which was still very strong, threatened to hurl them onto the rocks. The boat bobbed up on the crests of waves and then disappeared behind them as she skirted the base of the cliff in the hope of finding a low rock which they could come alongside. They spent two hours at this risky exercise, and then we saw them come back. It was quite impossible to land in such weather.

They had found that the whole coast was protected by a wall of smooth flawless ice which fell sheer into the open sea and was constantly battered by enormous waves. Several times as the motorboat tried to find a landing place it was almost flung on the rocks. It would have been madness to go on. The airplane also tried to make a reconnaissance, but the sea was so rough that it could not take off. At 4 P.M. we decided to go on, and the *Kista Dan* set off eastwards in a nightmarish landscape. The sea and sky ahead were both as black as ink,

and seemed to have joined together to form a single barrier to our route, and astern the rocks of the Scullin
Monolith faded into the mist. Only a few great white
icebergs shone in a strange light, like diamonds in their
murky setting. It was a magnificent but grim scene, a
deep depression hung over the ship and her passengers,
and we were all glad enough to escape to the warm
oasis of the messroom when the dinner bell rang.

For three days the ship steamed on eastwards
through strangely varied seas. In the same day we
passed from open water into thick pack ice, followed by
a field of pancakes or a porridge of slush, and this affected our progress very oddly. In some places there
were great crowds of icebergs packed together like the
columns in a cathedral and apparently blocking our
way. Then there were none, as though they had been
made to vanish by a magic wand. These masses of ice
probably meant that there was a snout of a great glacier
not far off. The icebergs had broken off in rectangular
chunks and some of them were quite enormous. We
sailed alongside one iceberg for nearly two hours, and
the captain reckoned it must be about six miles long. It
was the largest we saw during the whole voyage.

The weather was just as extraordinary and various,
chopping and changing, with clear blue skies, thick
fogs, snow squalls, high winds, calm spells, heat and

cold in turns, often in the course of a single day, in an absurd and unpredictable sequence.

But I was more worried by the course we were taking. Ever since we had left the Scullin Monolith we had been heading east, keeping pretty well on the same latitude (67° 46′ south), but, if anything, working gradually northwards. This course hardly seemed to agree with our plan of exploring the MacKenzie Sea and Sandefjord Bay to the southeast, to say nothing of landing on the Vestfold Hills in Princess Elizabeth Land. And in fact by the 27th we had already passed the longitude of the MacKenzie Sea and ought to have been heading due south. Our route was taking us farther and farther from our destination, and I kept wondering sadly if we were not abandoning our plans and heading for home.

Indeed, things did not seem to be going well on board, and it was clear that there was disagreement between Dr. Law and the captain and their two staffs. There were long discussions in the wardroom and mysterious conversations in the cabins. The Australians had long faces, and the Danish officers seemed unnaturally reserved. I said nothing, but Dr. Law could clearly read my thoughts and, being my neighbor at table, found it all the more difficult to conceal his embarrassment. Every day he used to tell me with a disingenuously cas-

ual air that we were on the point of heading southwards, and I felt that he had had more than enough of
cruising around the continent that we never saw.

Suddenly on the 28th the ship altered course. We
were then on the same parallel as the Ingrid Christensen
Coast (76° east), for which we now headed. We had
won the day. Everyone looked happy and all the strain
disappeared. Dr. Law explained to me that the trouble
during the last few days had been caused by two different points of view, both perfectly legitimate. He was
responsible for seeing that the mission did its scientific
work and was naturally concerned to see that the program was carried out. The captain, on the other hand,
was responsible for the safety of the ship and her passengers, and he refused to take risks which he thought
excessive. And indeed the state of the sea, the quantity
of young ice and the speed at which it had been growing during the last few days clearly showed that the
winter pack ice had already begun to form. And it was
getting late in the season. Captain Petersen dared not
risk seeing his ship stuck in the ice all winter. This would
have been extremely dangerous for, though we had
quite enough food, water and fuel for the voyage back
to Australia, there was not enough to last through the
winter.

In the end duty to science seemed to have overcome

the captain's prudence, though in fact the situation had changed in our favor. We were now on the meridian of the Vestfold Hills and quite close to the coast in a straight line. Moreover, a reconnaissance flight had just shown that between us and the coast there was only loose pack ice broken up with sheets of open water, so we should have no difficulty in reaching the shore; and we had come upon much less young ice during the past few days. The captain therefore felt he could take the risk so long as we didn't waste any time.

That night we celebrated the good news with a party in the mess. We sang Australian and Danish songs to the accompaniment of Dr. Law's accordion and Frank's fiddle, and large doses of whisky, brandy and aquavit soon washed away all traces of our recent gloom.

Then, suddenly, the officer of the watch burst into the mess shouting something I could not understand. Had there been another disaster? No, he was merely reporting an aurora australis, and we all rushed on deck to enjoy these natural fireworks that had been so unexpectedly and opportunely provided for our little party. It was quite the finest display we had yet seen and was a really wonderful sight. In the very clear but very dark sky an enormous bright-yellow plume shot up like flames from a volcano, spreading out into branches and festoons of changing colors and evanescent shapes. The whole icy landscape was brilliantly lit, and when I turned my head I saw another sight which I found comic but at the same time rather touching: on a great floe which lay almost alongside the ship there were a dozen emperor penguins standing quite still. They seemed to be watching the aurora australis as solemnly as we were. Or had they been attracted by our concert? Possibly, for it is known that they are very fond of music. To prove it to us Dr. Law fetched his accordion and began to play "The Dead Leaves," one of his favorite songs. There was no doubt that the penguins were interested; they stretched out their necks and turned their heads on one side as if trying to hear better. Little by little they waddled nearer to the ship's side, and then other penguins turned up which we had not seen before, and soon there were about twenty of them, an ecstatic little group only a few yards away. But it was bitterly cold, so in spite of the splendid aurora, which still blazed with all its lights, we had to leave off serenading the penguins and go down to our cabins.

On Monday, March 1, the weather was gray, bleak and overcast, with twenty degrees of frost and a light chilly breeze. We steered south-southeast towards the Vestfold Hills. By noon we had already reached latitude 68° 30′ south, having covered two degrees of latitude since the morning before. The ship made quite good headway through rather close pack ice, often broken by lakes of open water which helped us to gain time. It was still a question of whether we should reach the coast, as the pack seemed to be thickening as we went southwards, and we could not afford to spend much time plowing through it. Meanwhile Dr. Law, happy to be at work again, completed a detailed record of soundings with the aid of the ship's very convenient echo-sounding apparatus.

In the morning there did not seem to be a single sign in this desolate landscape, so colorless and empty, but gradually we began to see a few of the usual Adélies and some Weddell seals, and then the sun reappeared. At about 2 P.M. the ship came to a gentle stop almost touching the glittering wall of a huge iceberg that towered above us, and then she began to turn. Did this mean that we were turning back? I feared so for a moment, but then I discovered that we were only correcting our southerly course and that all was well.

The *Kista Dan* was now heading straight for the coast, which soon appeared on the horizon as a tall and ghostly cliff of ice scarred with crevasses. It was still twenty miles away, so the cliffs must be very high and the crevasses very deep to be so clearly visible at such a distance. Here the pack ice was very dense, but what worried the captain still more was the speed at which the young ice was freezing over. It seemed to us that we could see it spread hour by hour in the open spaces between the floes. Was there still time to reach the coast and to land?

The problem was serious, for we had done everything possible. It would be a tragedy if we had to turn back just as we were reaching our goal and it was already in sight. And what of the geodetic observations we had to make on this coast? Could we abandon them after having gone through so much to come so far? Every day we came more and more under the spell of this southern world, which called to us like a siren, a modern siren adorned with all the tinsel of science, who would keep us prisoners for long months if she could. The trap might close at any moment, and then it would be too late to escape. But when? Tomorrow? In a week? That was the crux of the whole problem. To stay or not to stay? I sympathized wholeheartedly with those who had to make the difficult decision.

But it seemed that the die was cast. Slowly, insensibly and apparently irresistibly the *Kista Dan* steamed on southward, as if the problem was no longer in our hands but had been taken over by Fate. As we neared the coast the circle of ice grew larger, enclosing in a crystal case the great dark-blue lake of open water, strewn with innumerable islets of all shapes and sizes known as the

Vestfold Hills. Two months ago I had not even heard their name, but I had been dreaming of them ever since. For each of us they were the symbol of the promised land. At nightfall we stopped fifty yards from the shore.

But our promised land turned out to be most unattractive. At five o'clock in the morning in the pale light of a hangman's dawn it looked to me very grim and desolate. The ship rolled heavily in a rough sea. A savage wind blew and swept squalls of snow across the deck. Round us stood the islands, bastions of black rock with snow on their crests and lighter-colored screes looking as if someone had shot out a large load of sand. When we examined a scree through field glasses we saw it was the guano deposited by great colonies of penguins. Between the islands lay a squadron of great icebergs, silent unmoving monsters which would become dangerous if there was a storm.

A whole program of work had been arranged. A geodetic team was to land on the mainland to determine the exact coordinates and measure the gravitational and magnetic fields. Then a party of naturalists was to land on the largest island to prospect hastily for minerals and to make a quick survey of the bird life. The airmen were to make reconnaissances, take air photographs and measure the radioactivity with a Geiger counter. These were the plans, but in the present weather there was no question of a landing even on the nearest island. The motor dinghy, which had been lowered in the hope of the weather's improving, filled with water in the swell and it took the whole morning to refloat her. Meanwhile the wind was driving the ship dangerously near the islands; her stern had grounded two or three times and her anchor had begun to drag. In order to avoid a disaster during the night Captain Petersen took her several miles out to sea and hove to.

Should we have to give up? I felt that the captain's one wish was to turn northwards and head for Heard Island, but poor Dr. Law was so unhappy at his persistent bad luck and at the prospect of failure that they agreed that he should have one more day of grace. But it was to be the last, and whatever the weather and whether the work had been finished or not the *Kista Dan* would start for home in twenty-four hours.

At dawn on March 3 we were blanketed in thick fog, the deck was deep in snow, but it was very mild, with only five degrees of frost, and the wind had dropped completely. It looked like clearing up, and the ship slowly returned to the position where she had lain the morning before. At ten o'clock the mainland team, consisting of Dr. Law, Dr. Gwynn, Jim Brookes, one radio officer and one meteorologist, started for the shore in the picket boat and we saw them disappear behind the islands. The weak sun came out shyly. It filtered through the haze and tinted the distant coastal glaciers with pale orange, but its rays had not yet reached the bay, the icebergs or the rocky islands, which were still the bleak color of the night, gradually changing to a delicate pastel blue.

About two o'clock the motorboat came back. The bad weather had prevented them from shooting the sun and establishing their triangulation point where they intended, so they had put the geophysicists ashore on the island nearest to the ship so that they could take magnetic readings. I got in the motorboat with a small party of naturalists and we set off in a violent snow squall to join them. Getting ashore was an appalling business, for the island was surrounded by broken and treacherous ice. The boat could not come at all close to the shore, and we had to be as nimble on our feet as tightrope walkers, for everything was deep in snow and one never knew whether one was stepping on a rock, a piece of loose ice or into a waterhole. On the island itself it was more cheerful. Snow kept falling, and the poor Adélie penguins in their rookery had all they could do with their little short wings to keep themselves from being snowed under. I found Jim Brookes and Elliott there, planted before their instruments and being gradually turned into snowmen. While I was filming the penguins they finished their magnetic readings, and soon we all returned to the ship, frozen, drenched and happy.

Dr. Law was bitterly disappointed at having failed to carry out his most important task of shooting the sun and setting up a triangulation point. But he persuaded the captain to put off our departure for another day. His perseverance was rewarded, for when we awoke next morning we found the sun shining brightly in a cloudless sky. Everybody was in high spirits, but the gods of the antarctic were evidently against us, for the motorboat obstinately refused to start and the airplane followed its example in spite of the desperate efforts of the mechanics. But we could not waste these few hours of fine weather, so a small survey party went off to the nearest island in a minute rowing dinghy, the only boat that still worked. Naturally this took rather a long time, and only a small number of men could be carried in so small a boat. But all the same Jim Brookes managed to establish a geodetic station in the best possible conditions, something which none of the previous expeditions had succeeded in doing. The magnetic observations he had taken on the previous day were very precise; so this important task had now been finally concluded, in spite of the abominable weather.[1]

---

[1] The exact geodetic bearing of the little island named Magnetic Island is 68° 33.2' south by 77° 54.2' east. The deviation is

Thin Edge of the World

Meanwhile the airmen had succeeded in mending their engine, taking off, making a reconnaissance and taking a number of air photographs. The job was done, and Dr. Law returned to the ship beaming with joy and the satisfaction of having done his duty. He must also have felt some pleasure at having thwarted the sinister forces which had seemed to be making a dead set at our expedition during the past few days. It was high time to make an end, for we had arrived at the last of our days of grace — the last hour of the last day, one might say. As soon as the airplane and the dinghy were safely on board, the sun hid itself, the snow began to fall again and the wind to blow just as if they had been waiting only for this signal.

At 1:30 P.M. on Thursday, March 4, 1954, the *Kista Dan* headed north in the direction of Heard Island. I stood for a long while on the quarter-deck watching the mainland fading in the mist — this antarctic mainland which had been one of the great dreams of my youth, a dream that had just been fulfilled after thirty years of waiting. And so I bade farewell to the continent where I had just passed some memorable hours and which I should doubtless never see again.

70° 10′ west, which is higher than might be expected, probably from local causes.

CHAPTER ELEVEN

The Journey Home

AS soon as we started it began to blow a gale from the northeast, the wind rising every hour. Our first night on the way home was the most terrifying of the whole journey. I doubt if any one of us will forget it.

The *Kista Dan* struggled gallantly against the storm, and Captain Petersen made desperate efforts to keep her head on to the waves, but by midnight the wind had reached a speed of ninety miles per hour or more, and it became quite impossible to control the ship. We had unloaded all our cargo at Mawson, and the ship was now riding high out of the water, and offering such a large area to the wind that it was no longer possible to resist its growing force. The limit had been passed: the ship no longer obeyed the helm and had begun to drift sideways through a sea bristling with icebergs — a mere toy at the mercy of the storm.

The situation was undoubtedly dramatic, but there was enough comic relief to prevent us from dwelling too much on the gloomier side of the picture. From what little I could see of my cabinmates' faces they did not look downhearted, and when they were thrown about by the ship's more savage movements their comments were full of wry humor. Our morale was not too low.

We could not possibly leave our bunks, but it was none too easy to stay in them, when the ship had a nasty tendency to chuck one out. We rolled more than it is possible to imagine. I reckoned from a curtain cord which was swaying ominously before my face that we were rolling at best forty-five and at worst fifty-five degrees, but next day I heard from the captain himself that the ship had sometimes heeled as much as seventy degrees. Few storms could have done better.

It was all the more uncomfortable because our bunks were built athwartships, so when she rolled seventy degrees one alternately stood on one's head and one's feet. It is true that I had become quite accustomed to being upside down when I used to practice yoga in the East. But yoga was not much help now, especially as there was such a ghastly shindy going on that it was quite impossible to concentrate on contemplation. I had enough to do to keep myself from being catapulted out of my bunk.

The hours passed, but still there was no lull in the storm, which blew as hard as ever. We were beginning to get used to the violent roll, but now it became even more unpleasant. Every now and then the ship lay right over on her side, stuck there as if she would never right herself again. Then slowly, very slowly, she raised herself, only to heel over once more on the same side. It was quite agonizing; these moments seemed to last forever, and each time I felt sure the ship would never right herself again — but stay on her side or even turn turtle. Mechanically, I counted the seconds before she righted herself, and so tried to reckon whether things were getting better or worse. I did not come to any conclusions, but at all events it kept my mind occupied during this interminably sleepless night.

Day dawned very slowly, its pale light revealing a scene of appalling confusion. It looked as if a hurricane had swept through the inside of the ship. Everything in our cabin was upside down. The drawers had slid out and emptied their contents, all our gear was adrift, smashed chairs lay overturned on the floor, which was awash with a tide of jumbled objects rolling from one wall of the cabin to the other. All through the ship one could hear doors banging, furniture crashing and broken crockery falling down the companion ladders or cascading through the galley and the wardroom. We made a laudable effort to get up and make some sort of order, but it soon became clear that this was too dangerous. Jim Brookes, who with Frank Morgan was now sharing my cabin, was yanked out of his bunk and flung against the cabin wall so hard that he was half stunned and had great difficulty in getting back to his bed. Better to wait, we thought.

We learned later that at three in the morning the airplane, which had made a reconnaissance on the day before, had totally disappeared. It had been lashed down onto a raised cradle on the quarter-deck and had been torn from its base by the wind and the waves which swept the deck. The cradle of six-inch oak with double iron braces had been smashed by the force of the wind.

In the morning the storm abated a little and after a good deal of acrobatics I managed to reach the wardroom. I could hardly see a thing. The portholes were so thickly coated with ice that only a faint light filtered through. The forward portholes were less exposed, and I could see through them. A monstrous sea was running outside. Huge waves reared up against the ship, high above the deck, in great walls of water. When one of them broke on the deck the ship shook from stem to stern, and I wondered how she could possibly stand up to such a battering. She rolled so heavily that the rail and a part of the deck disappeared under water which washed the portholes in the wardroom and the cabins. The deck and the rigging were entirely covered with a thick coating of ice, for the temperature was low (16° F. of frost) and the water froze as it touched the ship, till she was clad in a shell of ice.

The *Kista Dan's* situation was still serious. She went on heeling dangerously to starboard as she drifted through open or slushy water strewn with "bergy bits," growlers and icebergs. It was a miracle that we had not yet collided with an iceberg, though we had often banged into medium-sized chunks of ice, too small to be dangerous. In the afternoon the rolling suddenly became bearable and the ship at once hove to.

We had drifted blindly downwind since midnight, but some good angel had steered us past the enormous icebergs, which would certainly have destroyed us had we struck them. And now was it destiny, Providence or just a lucky concatenation of circumstances that had led us through to calmer waters? I could not tell. I was content to rejoice like my companions and to give thanks to the strange force which moves the world, the cosmic force which I feel within myself — the nameless power which has so often led me to safety.

The *Kista Dan* had hove to in the middle of a tongue of "brash" — a porridge of melting ice, more than a foot thick: an agglomeration of small bits of ice, shattered floes and crumbling icebergs. The weight of this scum of ice had calmed the sea as effectively as the oil used by the old navigators. The ship had straightened herself under her cloak of ice, but she still drifted southwest before the gale, which had not ceased to rage. We were still in danger of running into an iceberg, and the dull thud of bergy bits striking against the hull reminded us that the danger was by no means over.

This truce lasted for another thirty hours. The ship seemed to be motionless, but she still drifted westward in the center of this floating oasis. The wind still blew at more than sixty miles per hour, the sea was still high, but the waves were no longer breaking on the deck. It was a striking sight. Huge ice-covered waves rolled past, heaving high up above us. All the same, the ship came to life again, passengers began to show their faces at mealtimes and everyone set to work to repair the damage and clear up the shambles left by the storm.

On Saturday, March 6, at about noon, the wind fell suddenly, the sea went down: the storm was at an end. Captain Petersen was all in. For sixty hours on end he had not left the bridge. He had not had a single rest from the danger and responsibility he had to face. We owed our lives to his seamanship and remarkable knowledge of polar navigation.

But we could not rest yet. The vessel had suffered in the storm, as we soon learned, and she had drifted two degrees of longitude to the west. And at the height of the storm the captain had had to pump fifty tons of sea water into our fresh-water tanks to ballast the ship and reduce her windage. This emergency measure was unavoidable, but it had greatly reduced our supply of fresh water and we had to be strictly rationed. We should probably also have to touch at Kerguelen to fill up with fresh water, which would not now last till we reached Australia. I must admit that I did not mind this news; indeed, I was delighted at this unexpected chance of seeing my friends in the mission again. And I think that, apart from Dr. Law, who had other things to think of, most of the Australians were as pleased as I was at the thought of having to visit such a delightful haven as Kerguelen.

During the afternoon the *Kista Dan* slowly resumed her northeast course, but soon the mist became so thick and visibility so bad that we had to stop and wait for the weather to clear. On Sunday morning we steamed out of the great sheet of brash which had been our haven of refuge while the storm was raging. For two days we forged ahead at normal speed across a great lake of open water thinly strewn with floes and icebergs. During the afternoon of March 8 we again sighted the coast on the starboard bow, while to the west and north we could see a mass of pack ice extending out of sight. The storm had obviously kept us in the strip of open water along the coast, and we still had all the antarctic pack ice to cross. We wondered how wide it was, and how long it would take us to get through. We had not the slightest idea; and so late in the season there might still be unpleasant surprises. Our troubles were not all over yet.

Dr. Law was very worried because he did not know how long the return journey would take. When the Antarctic Division chartered the *Kista Dan* it was stipulated that she should be back at Melbourne by March 31, otherwise they would have to pay a heavy demurrage for every day's delay. He had therefore originally decided, much against his wishes, not to call at Kerguelen. This had been a great disappointment for all of us, but we had understood his reasons. A visit to Kerguelen meant a short rest from hard work among good companions with plenty of songs, good food, fine wines and the spirits which Australians enjoy so much but drink so little. Now we had lost almost all our water supply we were forced to visit Kerguelen and thus reconcile duty and pleasure. But for duty's sake we should have to cut our stay at Kerguelen and at Heard Island as short as possible. At Kerguelen everything would depend on the weather, which was always unpredictable, so we might hope to be able to stay there a little longer.

The Journey Home

The weather was as dreary as ever, gray and overcast, and the swell was so high that the messroom was again deserted. It was like the North Sea in winter. We crossed great sheets of young sea ice and towards evening came to an ominous forest of closely packed icebergs which must have been driven there by the gale. It was not long before we crossed the Antarctic Circle, and then we entered the pack.

Our journey through the pack ice took two days — less than we had expected. But it began very badly. Throughout the night the ship lay still. At five in the morning she got under way again, but after three hours of very slow progress she was stopped by the thickness of the ice. Things looked serious.

On each side of the ship the ice had piled up in remarkable hummocks. These mountains of ice are caused by storms piling up the ice until sometimes it reaches a height of seventy feet. Our hummocks were not as tall as this, but the floes were unusually thick, the blue ice was anything from six to twelve feet through. It snowed. A strong northeasterly wind swept across the ice at eighty miles per hour, raising so thick a blizzard that one could hardly see the ship's bow from the bridge. Close by us, on a large floe, three Adélie penguins huddled together, protecting themselves against the wind as best as they could. The blizzard had turned them into lumps of ice, and I wondered how they could survive. Not far away two crab-eating seals lolled nonchalantly on the ice, gradually being covered by snow. It was a perfect picture of antarctic desolation.

The ship itself seemed to be dead. Apart from the officer of the watch on the bridge, there was not a soul to be seen — everyone was asleep in his cabin recovering from the exhaustion of the last few days. No one could tell how long we should have to stay here, and the barometer was hardly encouraging. We should be badly handicapped without the airplane when it came to finding a way through the ice, but it could not have flown in the blizzard even if we had had one. In the afternoon there was a little life on deck and there was some talk of turning back on our tracks to look for a better route through the pack, but visibility was so bad that the captain soon gave up the idea.

Next morning the sky was still gray and overcast and it was still snowing, but the wind had fallen and the temperature had risen to 26° F. The sun was still hidden, but visibility had improved a little, and Captain Petersen gave the signal to go ahead. The *Kista Dan* moved slowly through the closely packed ice, which had, however, been broken up by yesterday's storm. There were plenty of channels of open water between the floes, so we made better speed. At about ten o'clock the sun began to show and the mists dispersed. Soon the sky was bright and clear. Once again I was astonished at the sudden change of weather in the space of a few hours — one of the strangest features of the antarctic climate.

With the sun, the ship came alive again, as if at the wave of a magic wand. The crew were at their stations and the passengers came out with their cameras trying to take a few striking photographs before we left the antarctic. There was plenty to photograph. The ship herself was the most sensational subject, for she had been entirely cased in ice by the freezing waves and spray which swept the deck all through the storm. Now that the sun had come out again the ship glistened with a thousand lights, like a floating jewel.

The ship was such a lovely sight that it seemed a pity to destroy such a wonderful castle of crystal, but the weight of all that ice made her top-heavy and hard to handle, besides blocking one's passage on deck. So the passengers and crew set to work to knock off the ice with picks, poles, hooks, shovels, knives and any other weapon they could lay their hands on. The layer of ice was very thick, especially on the rail, where there was more than six inches of it. There was ice all over the *Kista Dan*'s superstructure: the deck, the fo'c'sle ladders, the scuttles, the outside of the cabins and the crew's quarters, the derricks, the rigging, the winches and the chains — and it took a good day's work to hack off the sheets of translucent ice that sheathed the ship and throw the pieces over the side.

The sun shone at noon, so the captain was able to shoot it for the first time for several days and discover that our position was latitude 66° 17′ south, longitude 79° 27′ east.

By this time the pack was very loose, and in the afternoon we finally steamed right out of it. The sun was again clouded over and snow and mist swirled round the ship, which rose and fell to a long ocean swell. A few larger icebergs reminded us that we were still in the antarctic.

It took us three days to reach Heard Island — three wretched murky gray days without a single ray of sunlight. Then the thermometer rose gradually to freezing point, and then to 35° F. and 36° F. A new storm broke over us, almost as savagely as the storm from which we had just escaped. The wind blew at ninety miles per hour and a mountainous sea battered us dangerously and spread chaos once more inside the ship, making all rest impossible. On Sunday, March 14, at 8 A.M., we sighted Big Ben, the eleven-thousand-foot extinct volcano which towers over Heard Island. The peak seemed to be floating on the clouds which hid the lower slopes.

The coast of Heard Island is grim, especially in bad weather: bare black cliffs, falling sheer into the sea, broken only by the steep snouts of glaciers crawling down from the plateau hidden in the mist. The gale tore past, driving before it straggling clouds which were ripped into shreds of mist by the sharp peaks of rock; the sea tossed wildly and rain lashed the waves under a wan sky. It looked like a scene from Dante's Inferno. At midday we could see the Australian base and *Kista Dan* lay to in the slight shelter of a rocky cape. There was no anchorage where we could lie safely, and the captain had to keep the ship under way with her head to the wind. We tried to land, but once again the motorboat refused to start, and the whole afternoon was spent in repairing it. Night had almost fallen by the time the job was finished; it was raining in torrents, the sea was rougher than ever, and I preferred to wait till the next morning before going ashore.

After a very stormy night the sun showed its face again. By ten o'clock the weather had much improved and I was able to go ashore. There I was warmly welcomed by Mr. Bechervaise, the chief of the Australian mission, who took me all over the station. Although this station has to do the same kind of scientific work as our base at Kerguelen, it is very different in its conception and the way it has been designed. The numbers are very much smaller, nine or ten men instead of from forty-five to fifty, and they are all scientists or technicians, which avoids the difficulties we found at Kerguelen, where the scientists were outnumbered by workmen. The Heard Island team was much more closely knit; the scientists had to do all the manual work themselves, and they lived a much harder life than did their opposite numbers in Kerguelen. They therefore had a much better and more pioneering spirit.

The camp is also differently built. It consists of a lot of very small buildings of different kinds which seem to have sprung up at random to suit the casual fancy of the builders. Most of them are round or polygonal with conical roofs, so that the whole place looks like an African village or a traveling circus. Only the mess hut, the library and the laboratories are heated in winter; the private rooms never are, which must make them very bleak to live in, for the weather is much colder and more bitter than in Kerguelen. But the laboratories are excellently equipped, the radio and meteorological apparatus is first-rate, and the whole station can concentrate on its scientific work.

At 2 P.M. we went back on board the ship, leaving behind those few members of the 1954 mission who had

The Journey Home

come with us to the antarctic and taking with us those of the 1953 mission who were being relieved. Two hours later the *Kista Dan* got under way and plunged into the middle of a storm. The wind blew as hard as ever, as if it bore us a special grudge, and battered at us all the way to Kerguelen. We had another sleepless night. The three-hundred-mile voyage should have taken twenty hours, but with this savage gale in our teeth it took nearly double that time. In the small hours of dawn the weather at last agreed to improve, and it was almost fine as we steamed through the Pass Royale. By the time we moored in Port-aux-Français the sun was shining brightly, but the wind was as ferocious as usual.

But for some time there was no one to welcome us but the sun. Our friends did not expect us to arrive so early in the morning, and there was no sign of life at the base. Gradually figures began to appear from different directions on their way to the landing stage, and then we saw the *Gros-Ventre* leaving her moorings and making for the ship. The figures became clearer as they approached, and soon we recognized our old friends: Armengaud, the head of the mission, Redonnet and Dr. Millet, who gave us a friendly wave. A few minutes later they appeared on the deck of the *Kista Dan* and gave us a warm welcome.

Dr. Law hoped to get under way again that same

evening after taking on the twenty tons of fresh water we needed for the voyage to Melbourne, for he was more and more anxious lest we should return late and have to pay demurrage. And every day the interminably vile weather held us up and increased our delay. But we had more trouble ahead of us, for Armengaud told us of several disasters which would delay reloading with fresh water. The storm which we had suffered at sea had been just as savage at Kerguelen. The landing craft we had used in January had broken adrift, and the gale had flung it up high and dry on the shingle at the head of the bay. It did not seem to have been damaged, and was now being inspected, but we still had to wait for high tide. So even if the weather behaved itself — which the meteorologists thought unlikely — we could not possibly begin loading water until the next day. This was a great blow to Dr. Law, but since nothing could be done, he accepted the situation cheerfully, and the Australians all followed his example, glad that they could go ashore and enjoy themselves with an easy conscience. I was, of course, quite blasé about the attractions at Port-aux-Français, but I had a certain amount of official business to do and was glad we did not have to leave that same evening. So all was well.

I was very happy to be back in the old base where I had lived for so many months, and I was touched by the warm welcome M. Armengaud and my old friends gave me. They were all very interested in our adventures and kept me busy telling the story. M. Armengaud had good news for me. He told me that M. Sicaud had sent instructions from Paris to our consul general at Melbourne to look after me on my journey home. Then I went to our little hospital, where Dr. Millet and Père Jolissaint welcomed me like the prodigal son.

Bad weather prevented us still from getting on with loading fresh water. The landing craft had refloated the evening before, and we were glad to find it had not been seriously damaged. But a gale blew all through the night and the following morning, so there was nothing we could do. Fortunately the wind dropped early in the afternoon, and everyone, French and Australians alike, worked so feverishly that the forty tons of water were on board before nightfall. The sun set just as the landing craft finished its last trip. An official dinner on shore ended our short but pleasant stay at Kerguelen. Next morning at eight o'clock the *Kista Dan* weighed anchor, after giving several blasts on her siren to salute the French mission, which replied by banging away with small charges of explosive.

This was my last farewell to Kerguelen. I looked back at the cluster of buildings crouching under the radio masts. I followed the shore of the Courbet Peninsula, picking out Cormorant Point, the long beaches of the lower isthmus inhabited by sea elephants and Suzanne Point with its rookeries of gentoo penguins. When we had come through the Passe Royale I could just make out a tiny green smudge, which was the little island in Norwegian Bay, and far away to the north the long ribbon of silver coast, where I had enjoyed fraternizing with penguins. The last blurred outlines of the island faded into the haze, and that was the end of Kerguelen for me.

We had still twelve days at sea before we reached Melbourne — dull days when nothing happened — very monotonous after our adventures in the ice. Now there was nothing to see but the endless expanse of the Indian Ocean with its changing color, its gamboling porpoises, its sea birds and graceful albatrosses. But rough weather still dogged us, and the sea was high or moderate until we reached Australian waters. We were not really comfortable till we got to Melbourne. We were all rather exhausted after the excitement, hard work and sleepless nights that we had gone through; our evening song fests began to pall. We packed our bags, and each day we looked to see where we had got to on the chart, for the ship moved far too slowly for us, in our haste to reach the joys and disappointments on shore.

On March 31, 1954, the *Kista Dan* steamed into Melbourne, neatly finishing her long voyage on the very day that her charter expired. After all our disappointments and unexpected difficulties, the anxious race home was over and Dr. Law could rest in peace, content with the results which his patience, energy and pertinacity had achieved. Now, at last, a scientific station had been established in the Australian sector of the antarctic. Ten determined men were installed at Mawson, well-equipped for their scientific work. The expedition had completed its task and come back with a great deal of valuable scientific information. Moreover, we had suffered no casualties, and the material damage was no worse than was to be expected.

There was a holiday crowd on the dock to greet the *Kista Dan* as her crew moored her alongside as calmly as usual. There was a rush for the gangways, and the deck was invaded by a hustling pack of officials — cameramen, journalists and photographers, not to mention friends and relations of the Australians on board. The air was full of happy shouts of recognition and couples were colliding into one another's arms on every side. I suddenly felt very alone in this happy crowd. I no longer belonged to the friendly group of men with whom I had just spent three adventurous months. They had been very good to me, I had shared in their life, and become much attached to them. But now the adventure was over, the team was dispersing and its ephemeral spirit was breaking up into separate streams. Each man was claimed by his family, his friends and all the joys and sorrows of his past life.

I stayed in our deserted cabin putting my things together, and feeling, as I closed my trunks, that I was closing a chapter of my life. I began to feel the melancholy that comes at the end of an adventure, that fills those dead and static hours which divide the end of one part of one's life from the beginning of the next. But this always happens to the lonely and adventurous. And I belonged alone; I should always be lonely in the midst of friendship and love. But already I had turned my back on the past, and my spirit was tempted by the unknown adventures ahead.